ORIGINAL MGA

ORIGINAL
MGA

ANDERS DITLEV CLAUSAGER

PHOTOGRAPHY BY PAUL DEBOIS
EDITED BY MARK HUGHES

H&S

First published in 1993 by Bay View Books Ltd
Reprinted eight times
This edition published in 2023 by Herridge & Sons Ltd
Lower Forda, Shebbear, Beaworthy, Devon EX21 5SY

ISBN 978-1-906133-17-7
Printed in China

CONTENTS

Introduction 6
MGA Past & Present 8

MGA in Detail 16
- Chassis Frame 16
- Roadster Body 19
- Coupé Body 29
- Boot 32
- Roadster Interior Trim 35
- Coupé Interior Trim 39
- Weather Equipment 41
- Facia & Instruments 46
- Pushrod Engine 52
- Twin Cam Engine 60
- Exhaust System 63
- Ignition System 64
- Cooling System 64
- Carburettors & Fuel System 65
- Clutch 67
- Gearbox 68
- Propeller Shaft 70
- Rear Axle 70
- Rear Suspension 71
- Steering 71
- Front Suspension 72
- Brakes 72
- Wheels & Tyres 76
- Electrical Equipment & Lamps 79

Export Variations 84
Production Changes by Car/Chassis Numbers 86
Options, Extras & Accessories 89
Racing & Competition Equipment 94
Special Tuning 96
Identification, Dating & Production Figures 97
Colour Schemes 102
Buying Guide 106

INTRODUCTION

According to the introduction of a recent book about another famous make of car, the ideal archivist is someone who 'had everything in his head – right down to the colours of old models, their curious details, even their numbers, which would come to him before he had opened his dependable book' (Horst Mönnich: *The BMW Story – A Company in its Time*, 1991). While I am an archivist, I do not mean to be bombastic about it – but I hope this book at least is dependable.

This is my third contribution to the well-established and respected *Original* series. It has not been any less challenging and interesting to compile than the previous two. As archivist to the British Motor Industry Heritage Trust (BMIHT), it is my privilege to act as custodian of more records than any sensible person would ever wish to accumulate. Through writing books such as this, it is my intention to bring some of this information into a more practical form, and to make it accessible to a wider circle of enthusiasts. While considerable new research has gone into this book, the really interesting nuggets of information, as always, have had their comic habit of falling into my lap when I least expected them, while I was looking for something quite different – and which I most likely never found.

For a long time, the MGA has been one of the most sought-after British sports cars. It was already established as such when I first became involved with classic cars more than 20 years ago. Inevitably, there are many very knowledgeable people who were there before me. Being only too aware that, for many readers, authorship is synonymous with authority, I am grateful to the real pioneers of MGA lore who have been ready to share their accumulated experiences with me.

The odometer reading on Mike Ellman-Brown's Twin Cam roadster shows it to be the most youthful of several low mileage cars featured in this book, apart from being one of very few MGAs still in the hands of the original owner.

Part of the intention with this book was to search out a variety of different MGA models, in as near-original condition as is possible with cars more than 30 years old, and to take detailed photographs of them. A substantial list was compiled with assistance from the MGA Register of the MG Car Club, and our photographer Paul Debois was once again sent on a tour of the country. His two-pronged brief was both to take overall views of the chosen cars and to record minute and seemingly inexplicable details – requiring two very different approaches to photographic technique. The results are impeccable and Paul's work for this book has added a new dimension to the *Original* series.

Photographs were also contributed by my fellow Dane and toy car enthusiast Hans Hedegaard, an experienced car photographer who just happens to own two rather remarkable MGAs. Some gaps in the picture line-up were also filled by Andy Sargent, Geoff Barron and Graham Roberts, and somewhere within these pages there is one poor little snapshot of my own which just scraped through the editor's stringent quality control.

Of those who helped out with our photographic sessions, mention first and foremost must go to leading MGA specialists Bob West and Mike Horner of Horner & West Classic Cars, Pontefract, Yorkshire, for their immense help and patience during two hectic days of photography. Through them, we covered two complete cars, a partially restored Twin Cam coupé owned by Bob West, the ex-Nancy Mitchell car from the 1956 Mille Miglia, the prototype MGA coupé, and numerous mechanical components and optional extras.

The individual owners who generously allowed their cars to be used for photography were as follows: Reynold Finney (white 1500 coupé); Ian Chapman (white 1500 roadster); Graham Roberts (grey 1600 coupé); Mick Lambert (red 1600 roadster, during restoration); Clive and Chris Postles (blue 1600 De Luxe roadster); Mike Ellman-Brown (green Twin Cam roadster); Ian and Sue Bowen (red Twin Cam coupé); Nick Cox (white Twin Cam with hard top); Rob Otero (details from red Twin Cam coupé); and the afore-mentioned Hans Hedegaard (white 1600 Mark II De Luxe roadster and beige 1600 Mark II coupé) and Bob West (grey 1600 roadster, restored by David Atkins). I must also thank my colleague Richard Westcott, manager of the BMIHT's

The literature pack supplied with a late Twin Cam. Apart from handbook, service book and warranty document, there is the booklet 'Getting the best from your MGA Twin Cam', an accessory list, dealer lists for the UK and Europe, leaflets for Safety Fast *magazine, BMC underbody seal and radio installation, as well as the actual build card for the car which would normally not have been supplied to the customer. The original MG-stamped leather key fob is at the bottom, together with an interloper – a Schuco small-scale model of the MGA coupé.*

Heritage Motor Museum, then at Syon Park but now at Gaydon, for access to the Trust's sectioned Twin Cam coupé chassis. Ian Wallace, showing great sense of humour, kindly allowed his derelict 1600 coupé to serve as an extreme illustration of the ravages which rust can wreak.

While the photographs were being taken, I was completing the original draft of the text. The opportunity to use many of the original records, now kept on behalf of the Rover Group by the BMIHT, was of immense benefit, and it is only appropriate that I should record my thanks to my employers for preserving this material and making it available. I would also like to thank colleagues who assisted me in aspects of the research that had to be carried out. The finished manuscript was read and commented on by a number of people, some of whom attended a seminar to view and comment on the photographs. Those people who attended this seminar were Bob West, Nick Cox, Andy Sargent, Geoff Barron, Mike Ellman-Brown, Ian Bowen and Rob Otero. In addition, the manuscript was read by the following, mostly overseas: in the USA, Bob Vitrikas, Todd Clarke, Bill Gallihugh and Jonathan Stein – all leading MGA experts – as well as my good friend Frank Cangiano; in Denmark, by co-photographer Hans Hedegaard and another old friend, Knud Warnich, of whose Twin Cam I have many pleasant memories. Almost every one of these readers was able to bring some additional insight to bear on the subject, for which many thanks.

While I greatly appreciate the assistance rendered by so many experts, I can only stress than any errors and inaccuracies which may still be found in this book must be blamed only on myself.

In no small measure, my thanks are due to Mark Hughes and Charles Herridge. Mark, the editor of the *Original* series, supervised photographic sessions which I was unable to attend, and was his usual good-humoured and patient self throughout the sometimes protracted gestation period of this book. Charles, my publisher, and his wife Bridgid are delightful people to write for.

It is necessary to add a word about nomenclature. I have used the word 'roadster' throughout to describe the open MGA model, in preference to the equally valid 'two-seater' or 'tourer' – but a 'convertible' the car emphatically is not. The expressions 'left-hand' and 'right-hand' always refer to the way they would be used if looking at the car from the rear (or if sitting in the driver's seat). Finally, I have applied the title 'De Luxe' in the common way, referring to *all* pushrod-engined cars fitted with four-wheel disc brakes and centre-lock disc wheels. In adopting this convenience, I am not disagreeing with the real experts who assert that MG never called these cars 'De Luxe' (at least not the 1600 Mark II so equipped, *pace* Mike Ellman-Brown).

There have been many books previously written about MGs in general, and a few about the MGA in particular. My work has in no small measure been inspired by those who travelled down this road before me, and I shall feel flattered if, in turn, somebody else takes up the baton and continues research into detailed aspects of the MGA. After all, while I hope this book brings some new information to the general reader and MGA enthusiast, I do not really expect it to be the last word on the subject.

Whether you already know and love MGAs, or whether you still remain to be converted, I hope that you will find enjoyment as well as bare facts in the pages that follow.

Anders Ditlev Clausager
Birmingham, October 1992

MGA PAST & PRESENT

This Old English White 1500 roadster, now owned by Ian Chapman, is an extremely original low mileage car with left-hand drive to North American specification. It spent most of its life in Texas before being re-imported to the UK.

Reynold Finney's coupé is a 1500 model – the small single rear lamps are the giveaway. This Old English White car has the correct two-tone interior with a combination of red and white trim parts. The luggage rack is a popular addition on any MGA.

I must have been all of six years old. We were a Morris family and my father had taken delivery of a new Oxford in 1955. Some months later, during a visit to Copenhagen, we were shown around the factory of DOMI, the company which imported all Nuffield products to Denmark. There in a quiet corner of the assembly hall stood a brand-new bright red MGA, possibly one of the first to arrive in my native country. My older brother and I – both equally car mad at that time – were allowed to sit in the car.

It has since been my privilege and pleasure to know and drive several MGAs, if not – alas! – to own one. So if that particular love affair remains unrequited, that first encounter of an impressionable child may nevertheless have sparked off my life-long fascination with the octagon.

The concept of the MGA went back to 1951 when MG's chief designer, Syd Enever, produced an all-enveloping body for George Phillips' TD to run at Le Mans. The car did not do very well in the race and has long since disappeared, but the basic shape is instantly recognizable as the precursor of the MGA. There was, however, one problem with the car: the driver sat too high and too exposed because of the high TD chassis frame. Enever wanted to develop a new streamlined MG sports car to replace the T-series, so he sketched out a new chassis with the side members moved well outboard to give the lower seating position required. The prototype was fitted with a body developed from that of the Le Mans TD, but it still had the XPAG type engine which required an unsightly bulge in the bonnet.

Mike Ellman-Brown's Twin Cam roadster was the last example of this model to be made, and is all original as supplied to him when new in 1960. The car was finished in a non-standard colour, Woodland Green, to special order.

This sectioned Twin Cam coupé is possibly the car which was displayed at the 1958 Earls Court Motor Show, although it originally had a complete body. It is now in the BMIHT collection at the Heritage Motor Centre, Gaydon. Although much of the finish is non-standard, the car gives a useful insight into the anatomy of a Twin Cam.

This 1600 roadster was restored by David Atkins.

When this prototype was finished in 1952, MG had a new master in the shape of Leonard Lord, chairman of the newly-formed BMC group which had brought Austin and Nuffield together. John Thornley, MG's general manager, and Enever showed their new baby to Lord, who was just about to sign a contract with Donald Healey to make the Austin-Healey sports car and did not look upon the new MG with any favour. So the project was initially turned down. Only a year later Lord changed his mind and allowed Abingdon to go ahead with the new car. This delay had one fortunate result: by late 1953, the new 1½-litre BMC B-series engine was ready for production, and this was quickly incorporated in the new MG sports car.

The introduction of what was initially called the UA-series was planned for 1955. However, the car was in all respects so new compared with previous MG designs that the decision was made to change its name to MGA, signifying that it was 'the first of a new line' (to quote the original publicity material). BMC was also preparing a return to motor sport, and the decision was taken to show off the new model in advance of introduction by running three cars in the 1955 Le Mans 24 Hours. These were in many respects different from the production cars – although they looked just the same – and were known as the EX.182 models. Of the three cars, one crashed but two finished the race and gave a sufficiently good account of themselves.

The production car appeared in the autumn of 1955 in time for the London Motor Show – the actual launch was at the Frankfurt Motor Show – and was given an enthusiastic welcome. Despite being a radical change from MG's traditional square-riggers, the shape of the MGA proved itself when the new model was found to be

Another 1600 model in Dove Grey, this coupé owned by Graham Roberts has a known history from new and is very original throughout. It is one of the few cars featured in this book to have the standard bolt-on disc wheels with hub caps.

capable of almost 100mph. From the start of the project, Thornley and Enever had argued that they needed a streamlined body and a full 1½-litre engine to continue MG's success in the vital American export market, and they were proved to be absolutely right. The MGA went on to become the best-selling British sports car in the USA up to that time.

From an early stage there were plans for a higher-performance model and designs were prepared for twin overhead camshaft engines, one such car running in the 1955 Tourist Trophy race. The production version of the MGA Twin Cam appeared in 1958, and apart from the special engine featured Dunlop disc brakes all round and centre-lock disc wheels. It was rather more expensive than the standard model but offered a 115mph top speed – sensational for a 1½-litre sports car in the 1950s. On the debit side, it could be temperamental and unreliable if neglected, and remained a limited production specialist model.

The standard model continued with little change until 1959, the original roadster having been joined by a coupé in September 1956 (a body style also offered on the Twin Cam). But in the summer of 1959 the original car – subsequently usually known as the MGA 1500 – was replaced by the MGA 1600. The engine was increased in size from 1489cc to 1588cc, the same as the Twin Cam, reflecting the fact that the 1600cc class was replacing the 1500cc class in motor racing. The 1600 model was also fitted with Lockheed disc brakes on the front wheels, as well as several other smaller changes, many of which were implemented on the Twin Cam.

In 1960 the Twin Cam went out of production, and soon after MG introduced the option of Dunlop four-wheel disc brakes and centre-lock disc wheels (as used on the

Twin Cam) on the 1600, a variant which has become known as the De Luxe model. It seems likely that this was a ploy to use up surplus Twin Cam components. Originally built to special order only, by 1962 the De Luxe cars were being built in substantial batches for the US market, although overall production remained low with a mere 395 cars of this type being built.

The American export market slumped badly in 1960-61, and for a time the Abingdon production lines lay almost idle, while some American-specification MGA cars held in stock were converted and sold in other markets. While the eventual MGA replacement (in the form of the MGB, introduced in 1962) was coming along nicely in the development shop, MG introduced a final MGA derivative to shore up falling sales in the USA. The 1600 Mark II featured an even bigger engine, of 1622cc. Unfortunately, this capacity was just the wrong side of the 1600cc class barrier in motor racing, but, from the production point of view, it was conveniently the same size engine which would soon be standard in BMC's family saloon models. The revised MGA was identifiable by a new radiator grille and new rear lamps, neither of which was an improvement over the original. In early 1962, the 100,000th MGA, a 1600 Mark II roadster specially finished in metallic gold paint, left the production line and was proudly displayed at the New York Motor Show. Such a production figure was unheard of among sports cars. Soon after, MGA production ran down and the new MGB model took over.

After the initial 1955 race appearances, BMC decided to concentrate their competition efforts on rallying, and for a few years MGA works rally cars appeared regularly on the European scene. Nothing very spectacular was achieved, although

A 1600 (Mark I) De Luxe is one of the more unusual variations. This Iris Blue roadster is owned by Clive and Chris Postles. It should be mentioned that this car is a converted left-hand drive model re-imported from the USA, but all the work done on the car is to original specification and a very high standard. The blue hood and sidescreens were unique to this paint colour.

This Twin Cam coupé is the early type with 1500-style body and the colour is Orient Red. The car is owned by Ian and Sue Bowen but would tempt the author, not only for its registration mark!

Nancy Mitchell, who drove either an MGA or an MG Magnette, became European Ladies' Rally Champion in 1956 and 1957. From 1959 to 1962, works teams of MGAs were run in the American Sebring 12 Hours, Twin Cams the first two years, then De Luxe coupés. Ted Lund raced a very special Twin Cam at Le Mans in 1959, 1960 and 1961, officially as a private, MG Car Club supported venture but with extensive factory support behind the scenes. For the 1960 race, the car was altered to become a fastback coupé. The final fling of the MGA's works competition career came in 1962 when a 1600 Mark II De Luxe coupé gained class wins in the Monte Carlo and Tulip Rallies. Private owners, of course, have continued to race and rally MGAs to this day.

During the 1960s, the MGA was largely overshadowed by the new MGB, but when interest in classic cars began to mushroom in the early 1970s, the MGA soon became a favourite with enthusiasts once again. The Twin Cam models were particularly sought-after and the rare De Luxes carved their own niche, but MGAs of all models became, and remain, extremely popular. The large numbers preserved worldwide created the market for a flourishing trade in remanufactured parts. Prices inevitably began to escalate, especially in the boom years of the late 1980s, when it became common practice to re-import cars from the USA to Britain, with many ex-US cars also finding a ready market in Europe or Australia.

The appeal of the MGA is due to many factors. Mechanically, it is simple, robust and reliable. The performance is perfectly adequate. The handling and roadholding are among the best of any 1950s sports cars. It is a comfortable and easy car to drive. And it is pretty, its rounded, flowing lines holding a particular appeal for the 1990s when aerodynamic or organic shapes are again coming back into fashion. From every point of view, the MGA is an utterly practical proposition, yet capable of giving the owner and driver immense pleasure.

The 1600 Mark II can be distinguished by its radiator grille. This roadster owned by Danish enthusiast and photographer Hans Hedegaard is the De Luxe model equipped with Dunlop disc brakes on all wheels and the Twin Cam style centre-lock disc wheels. The indicator lamps in front of the doors are a legal requirement in Denmark, and in this case are of the appropriate type for a car of this period. The door-mounted mirror is a contemporary after-market accessory.

Hans Hedegaard's other MGA is almost as rare as the De Luxe roadster – a 1600 Mark II coupé, painted in the very unusual colour of Alamo Beige. Like his roadster, it is fitted with additional indicator lamps and a door mirror, probably a contemporary Lucas type.

MGA IN DETAIL

The skin and bones. This Twin Cam coupé body is neatly separated from its chassis and engine. The widely-spaced side members and the goalpost or bridge assembly behind the engine are evident. Note also the crossmembers at the rear, the support rails for the floorboards and the battery cradles.

The front end of the Twin Cam chassis shows the Dunlop disc brakes, the steering rack (mounted slightly further forward than on the standard model) and the anti-roll bar. Still missing on this car are the outer horns for mounting the front bumper.

CHASSIS FRAME

The chassis frame was in many ways an unusual and interesting design. To permit a lower seating position and thus overall height compared to previous MG models, the fully boxed-in side members were swept out between the axles, almost creating an American-style perimeter frame. Extra rigidity in the scuttle area was provided by the goalpost assembly of vertical pillars with a connecting cross bar, and this was further braced by inclined box section members to front and rear. Across the front axle line was a substantial welded-in bridge piece, incorporating the two front engine mountings and with an inverted cup overhanging each side member, housing the coil springs. The front end chassis frame extension was a separate unit which was bolted on to the main frame. The front extension had a tubular crossmember and two angled bumper support brackets.

There was a curved tubular crossmember just behind the engine, a box section crossmember behind the gearbox which incorporated the rear engine mounting, and a tubular crossmember between the front mounting points of the rear springs. Floorboard rails were fitted inside the chassis in the areas defined by these three central crossmembers. Longitudinal floorboard rails on either side of the centreline of the chassis also gave support to the gearbox cover and the propeller shaft tunnel. Two battery cradles were hung from the third tubular crossmember and the rearmost transverse floorboard rails. A channel section crossmember was found above the rear axle, and a final tubular crossmember across the very back end of the chassis.

There were thirteen main body mounting points, six each side, as follows: on the front extension assembly, to the side of the

From this angle, the heelboard shows up clearly. This chassis has the full complement of four horns for mounting the front bumper. The front drum brakes may just be seen, and the position of the ignition coil on top of the dynamo is another clue to this car being a 1500 model.

On this 1500 rolling chassis, the floorboards have been fitted in place but have yet to be painted their correct black. However, the shape and position of the floorboards show up better in the natural wood colour.

goalpost assembly, on the side member in the area of the door front pillar, by the third tubular crossmember, on the crossmember over the rear axle, and at the rear end of the chassis. Finally, the body was bolted to the top of the goalpost assembly. Plywood was used for the two toeboards, the four floorboards in two pieces on either side of the tunnel, and the one-piece heelboard or rear ramp. The gearbox cover stretched well aft of the remote control mounting, leaving only a short propeller shaft tunnel.

The entire chassis frame was finished in black petrol-resistant chassis paint. Gearbox cover and propeller shaft tunnel were painted black on the outside (the top) and were sprayed with sound-deadening Flintkote material on the inside. The floorboards, toeboards and heelboard were painted black.

The differences between the different MGA chassis frames concern only those areas where the basic frame design had to be adapted slightly. For instance, the different brake pipe runs on the Twin Cam and De Luxe models meant that pre-drilled holes for pipe clips were in different locations. These models also had a different starter switch bracket mounting. Twin Cam type chassis had the front crossmember pre-drilled for oil cooler pipes, and additional holes to facilitate sump removal. The engine mountings were different, and the body mounting points on the top of the goalpost assembly were differently located. The radiator and steering rack were further forward. The fuel pump mounting bracket was larger and had different holes. The same part number (AHH 5708) was quoted for the Twin Cam chassis frame, and for the chassis of the 1600 Mark I De Luxe.

There were few modifications to the chassis frame and associated parts, but on the 1500 from car/chassis 61504 the right-hand toeboard and gearbox cover were modified to give clearance to the starter motor in the higher position introduced with the start of the 15GD series engine. From car/chassis 66574 the front extension was altered to facilitate the installation of the optional anti-roll bar then becoming available. This modification was introduced on the Twin Cam from car/chassis 2275, and from this point on the anti-roll bar was standard on the Twin Cam. On 1600 Mark II models, from car/chassis 100352, seat belt anchorage mounting points were incorporated,

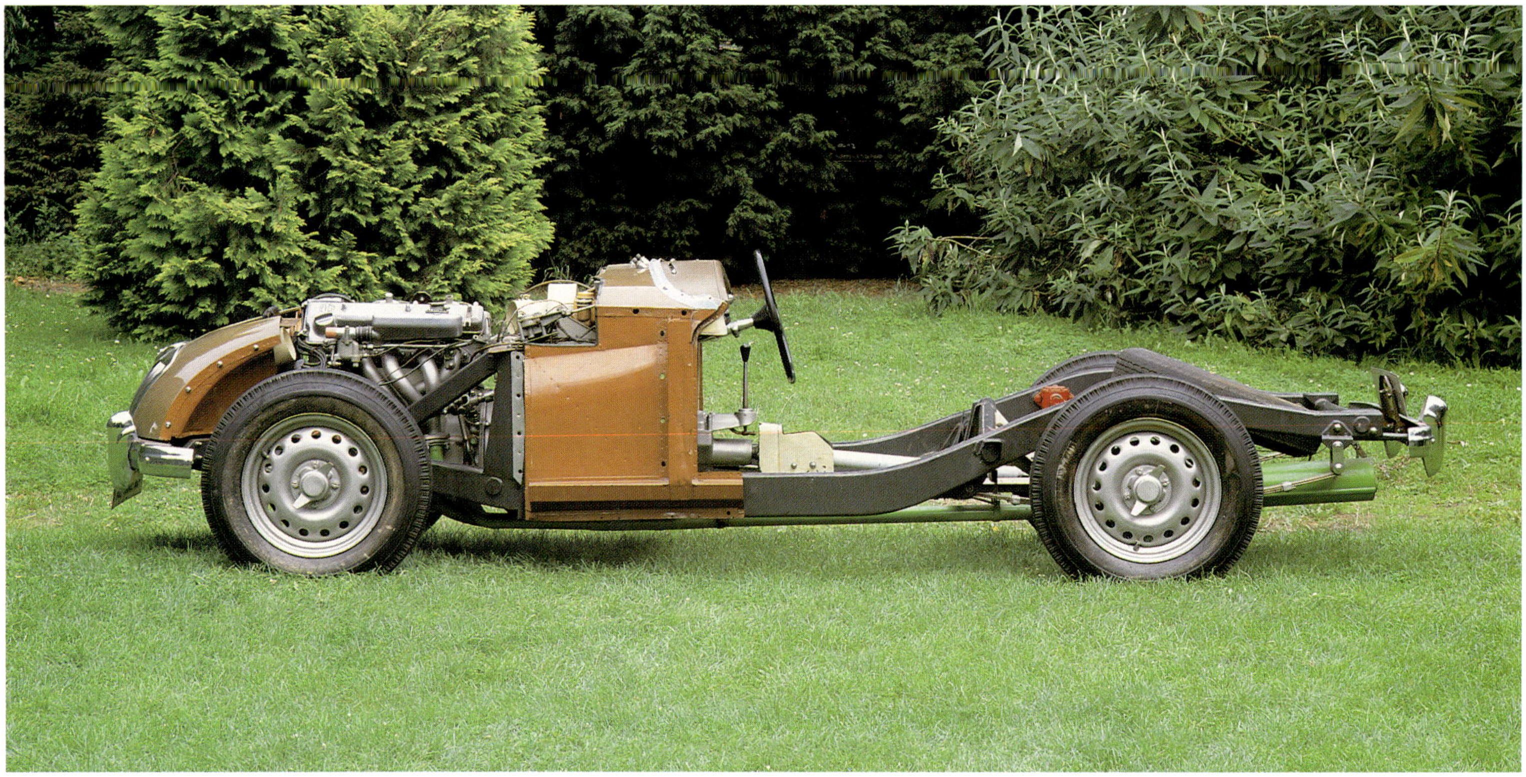

In side view, this sectioned Twin Cam coupé clearly shows how the chassis starts to sweep up over the rear axle well in front of the axle, and the inner scuttle structure is revealed.

From this angle, the section of the body sill can be seen, together with the door hinge pillar and some detail of the front suspension.

including one on each chassis side member and one on each side of the propeller shaft tunnel. The third mounting points were under the rear tonneau panel (roadster) or on the rear wheel arches (coupé). The anchorage points could be retro-fitted on all earlier MGA cars, using special kits made available by BMC at the time.

It is worth noting that the chassis number was at least sometimes stamped on the frame; cars have been reported both with and without the number stamped in. The location is the horizontal top surface of the box section crossmember at the rear of the gearbox, on the right-hand side of the gearbox cover tunnel, approximately three to six inches from the tunnel. The number stamped here will simply be the five- or six-figure number without any prefix (on the Twin Cam models, three or four figures only). Some instances have also been reported of export cars to certain destinations having their car/chassis numbers stamped in by the importers to comply with local requirements, although in such cases the number was more likely to

Allowing for the fact that almost every single colour is incorrect, this useful illustration shows the bulkhead layout of a left-hand drive car. From left behind the heater are control box, fusebox, flasher unit, flasher relay, master cylinder box and wiper motor. Note also the Twin Cam style air filters and the radiator with remote header tank behind the engine. The cam cover in the foreground has been partially cut away.

One or two controls are missing from this facia and the colour finishes are not correct. As this is a coupé, the facia panel goes around the corner at each extremity. The car has an adjustable steering column. Note the shape of the chassis crossmember under the gearbox extension, and the rails for the floorboards and propshaft tunnel.

In case you wondered, the exhaust should not be lime green and the shock absorbers should not be red! These are original Road Speed tyres. The rearmost body mounting points are in the foreground.

be stamped into a part of the body than into the chassis. The boot floor was one location. This certainly happened in Denmark, possibly also in other European countries.

MGA chassis frames were well-made from comparatively heavy-gauge steel, but will eventually rust. It is predominantly the centre section of the chassis which is affected. Floorboard rails and battery cradles are early victims, but the side members from goalpost to the third tubular crossmember are also affected. Stress-induced hairline cracks may occur at the top of the goalpost where it is joined by the angled bracing members from the front.

The only other variation of the chassis frame was that police specification cars could be fitted with larger battery cradles, but this was extremely unusual and never mentioned in the Service Parts Lists.

Roadster Body

The MGA's body was of all-steel construction, except that doors, bonnet and boot lid were skinned in aluminium. The

Details worth looking at on this freshly-painted Orient Red 1500 body include the front valance panel with four holes for the bumper mountings, the central starting handle hole, the radiator duct valance, the shape of the grille aperture, and the size of the sidelamp apertures.

bodies were made by Morris Motors Bodies Branch at Coventry. The roadster and coupé bodies were fundamentally of similar design, but the unique features of the coupé body are dealt with in the next section.

The important structural members of the body were the sill reinforcement and door pillar assemblies on each side, often referred to as the F-sections because of their shape. The front end of the body was composed of the front side assemblies which formed the sides of the engine bay and inner front wings, with the front end assembly or bonnet surround panel – usually known as the front shroud – on top, over a reinforcing frame of top-hat sections. The two sides of the body were linked by the transverse front bulkhead assembly incorporating the horizontal shelf behind the engine, the radiator duct panel and the front valance.

At the rear, the rear tonneau panel assembly incorporated the rear shroud or boot lid surround panel, the inner rear wings, and the inner rear quarter panels behind the doors. The rear shroud was also mounted over a top-hat section frame, and the rear valance or tail panel was integral with the shroud. The other main panels forming the rear structure were the boot floor and the transverse rear bulkhead between the tonneau area and the boot. This bulkhead had an aperture for the spare wheel. The tonneau floor was the battery access hatch held in place by two painted Dzus fasteners (five on the very early 1500 models). The front and rear wings were bolted on, with grey PVC piping in the joints.

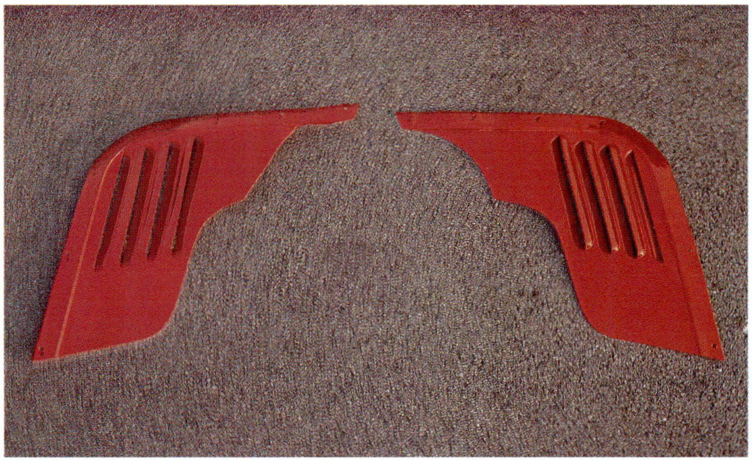

Unique to the Twin Cam and 1600 Mark I De Luxe are these removable louvred panels from the front inner wings. Note the difference in shape and size between left-hand and right-hand side panels.

Modifications to the body included the sill finishing strips which were added on the 1500 model from car/chassis 19949. Each strip was fitted with five bolts from the inside so there were no visible outside fixings. Splash plates were fitted behind the wheels in both front and rear wings, but from car/chassis 29935 splash plates were also fitted in front of the rear wheels.

An important modification occurred at the time of the Twin Cam's introduction. To give the necessary clearance for the longer and taller engine on this model, the curvature at the front of the bonnet was increased. The revised bonnet was fitted to all MGAs thereafter, but there was no change to the part number and it is not possible to establish at which point in the pushrod engine car production run the new bonnet was introduced. The difference is obvious enough if you have an early 1500 model parked next to any of the later cars, but can otherwise be difficult to spot. The bonnet frame and the position of the bonnet prop were altered on the revised bonnet. Bonnets are fully interchangeable with the proviso that an early 1500 bonnet will not fit a Twin Cam.

The Twin Cam body was originally mostly like the 1500's, but from Twin Cam car/chassis 592 the front inner wings of this model were fitted with louvred detachable access panels. These were found on the 1600 Mark I De Luxe models, but not on Mark IIs. Detail differences on Twin Cam bodies included the horizontal shelf behind the engine, a shorter radiator duct panel as the radiator was further forward, and also the radiator and air duct brackets.

The original 1500-type bodies had body

Three different frontal aspects are found on MGAs. The 1500 (top) and early Twin Cam models are distinguished by their small sidelamps which always have all-white lenses. The later Twin Cam models (centre) and the 1600s have bigger sidelamps with separate bulbs for the flashing indicators, and part amber lenses (all-white on North American and some other export cars). Finally, the 1600 Mark II (bottom) has a different grille with recessed bars. The parking position for the wipers is always in front of the driver on both LHD and RHD cars.

From the rear, the type and position of the rear lamps is the most important point to identify the different models. On the 1500 (top) and early Twin Cam, small single all-red Lucas rear lamps are found. On the later Twin Cam (centre) and 1600, there are additional separate flashing indicators and new plinths for the rear lamps and indicators. On the 1600 Mark II (bottom), the all-new combined lamp units are found on the rear shroud panel below the boot lid. The additional boot lid badges on the Twin Cam and 1600 Mark II models are worth noting. On this Mark II, the small triangular enamel badge was added by the Danish importer when the car was new.

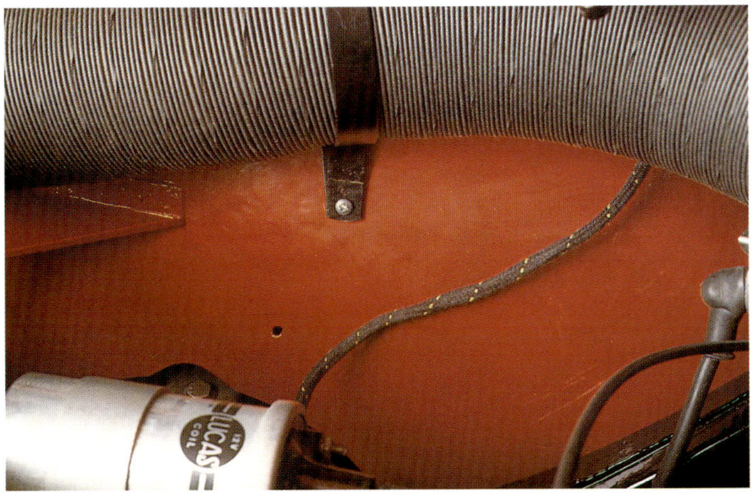

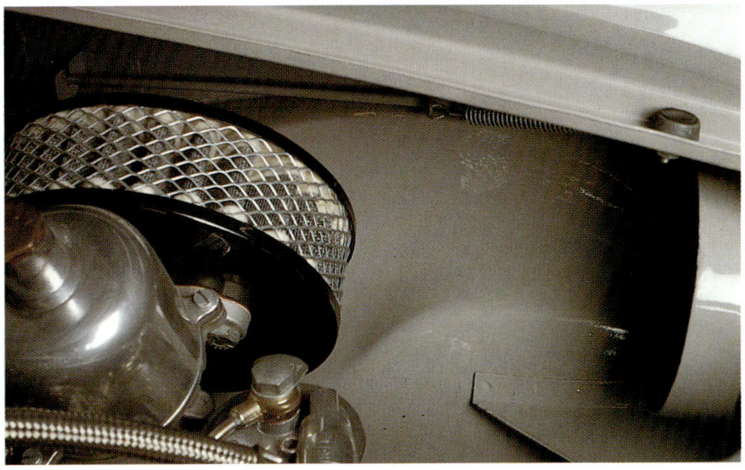

Some little-documented panel changes occurred early in the MGA's life. The original 1500 right-hand inner front wing (red car) was like this, but on later models (grey car) a dimple was pressed in the wing, to accommodate the Twin Cam front carburettor and air filter.

numbers with five figures and without any prefix, the body number being stamped on a small vertical tag to the right of the centre of the bulkhead behind the engine. Twin Cam and coupé bodies had numbers allocated in batches of 1000 taken from the main sequence. For details please refer to the section dealing with identification later in this book. Although the 1600 bodies were very little modified, the introduction of the 1600 model saw the start of a new series of body numbers with the number being prefixed by the letter B. The 1600-type body was also introduced on the Twin Cam model.

The major modification introduced with the 1600 model were new front wings, to suit the larger sidelamps. There was also a new type of rear lamp plinth to accommodate the separate rear flashers. On the 1600 Mark II, the rear wings were modifed as the rear lamps were moved to horizontal plinths on the rear shroud below the boot lid. On all cars the rear lamp plinths were painted body colour. On the 1500 and early Twin Cam models, the plinths had black PVC gaskets, changed to grey on the 1600 and later Twin Cam models. The 1600 Mark II originally had rubber gaskets, but from car/chassis 101353 these were replaced by lengths of cream Prestik material.

The bonnet and the boot lid were both fitted with reinforcing frames, consisting of two longitudinal members with X-bracing. Both bonnet and boot lid had a wood stiffening batten and anti-drumming felt strip sandwiched between frame and skin, at the front of the bonnet and at the rear of the boot lid. The body colour internal bonnet release was fitted under the facia on the left-hand side of the car. A safety catch was fitted on the left-hand side of the bonnet, and this and the bonnet lock were painted body colour. The bonnet was supported by a black prop, fitted to the bonnet at the front, with a black clip at the rear. On the original flat bonnet the prop was fixed centrally at the front. On the later curved bonnet, the prop was on the right-hand side on pushrod cars, and on the left-hand side on Twin Cams. The two bonnet hinges at the rear were painted body colour. The closed bonnet rested on ten rubber buffers fixed in the lip of the bonnet

Similarly, the left-hand inner front wing was changed. The early red 1500 has a small dimple to clear the air filter. The grey 1600 has a larger kidney-shaped depression, making room for the heater air intake hose of the Twin Cam model.

The red car (above) has the early 1500 flat bonnet. The grey car (right) has the later bonnet with more curvature, introduced to clear the Twin Cam engine.

The bonnet release pull, found on the left-hand side under the scuttle.

The boot lid release, on the left-hand side in the tonneau area, is very similar to the bonnet release and also painted body colour.

It is easier to identify the two different bonnets from the underside. The red bonnet (facing page) is the early flat type, the grey bonnet (right) the later type. On the later bonnet, the body prop is hinged further out, and the X-brace of the frame and the crossmember (which is more curved) are further back. On the later bonnet, there are additional bracing pieces to the frame on either side halfway back, and a small cut-out in the frame just behind the prop hinge point, to clear the Twin Cam carburettor. Note the body-colour hinges, bonnet lock and safety catch, and the black prop and clip. The black line visible below the lock is the timber reinforcement. Neither of these bonnets have the thick horsehair pad which rests on the radiator when the bonnet is closed.

This thick black horsehair or felt pad should be found under the bonnet of all pushrod-engined cars, closing the gap between radiator header tank and bonnet. On the 1600 shown, the bonnet prop seems to be on the wrong side but is the correct black colour. The bonnet lock and safety catch are correctly painted body colour.

aperture. Pushrod cars had a black horsehair pad glued to the underside of the bonnet at the front.

The boot lid also had an internal release, painted body colour and fitted in the left-hand bottom corner of the rear bulkhead just above the floor of the tonneau area. There was thus no external boot handle or lock. The two boot lid hinges were body colour. The boot lid was supported on a black prop fixed to the lid in the rear left-hand corner, with a black clip in the diagonally opposite corner of the boot lid. A rubber sealing strip was pushed into the lip round the edge of the boot lid aperture.

Each door was supported on two body coloured hinges, fitted with four crosshead screws to the door pillar and the door respectively. The hinges were modified on the 1500 model during 1958 to increase the door opening, and the modified type of hinge was identical on both sides of the car; the original hinges had been handed. The roadster had no external door handles, the lock being activated by a plastic-covered pull cord reached from inside the door pocket. In early 1958, the method of attaching the cable to the door lock lever was improved, as the cable was modified to incorporate the end bracket. There was a single rubber/Furflex door seal around the inside of the door opening, in one piece and fitted with chrome-plated end caps at the top front and rear. The Furflex was originally colour-coded to match the trim, but from the start of the 1600 model the colours were reduced to black and red.

The radiator grille had a chrome-plated brass case or frame, fixed with two studs at the bottom and two at the top, on brackets inside the case. The false nosepiece bore an enamel MG badge. The badge had a white

The roadster differs from the coupé in having a much simpler door lock (activated by pull cable) and two buffers (instead of one) on the door post.

The 1600 Mark II roadster featured a revised water channel at the top of the door shut pillar. This illustration also shows the rubber/Furflex door seal with chrome-plated end cap, the simple door lock striker and the upper of the two rubber buffers for the roadster door.

All MGAs except 1600 Mark II models have this style of radiator grille, with the bars following the line of the bonnet and shroud panel. The nosepiece is original but has been slightly damaged.

The 1600 Mark II models have the bars recessed at the bottom, with an extra surround piece inserted between the grille casing and the bars. It can be seen how the bars either side of the centre rib are angled towards the outside of the car, and how the piping between casing and shroud continues round the bottom corner and stops about two inches in on either side.

Surprisingly, many reproduction parts for the MGA are quite different from the originals. Of these two bumpers, the reproduction is on the left, the more subtly shaped original on the right.

background, with the black border and letters outlined in chrome. The nosepiece was held in place by a bolt from the back of the badge. The grille had 14 vertical stainless steel bars on either side of the centre rib, the outermost bars being hardly visible except at the top. The section of the grille bars was angled towards the outside of the car on either side of the centre. There was grey PVC piping between the grille frame and the front shroud. The piping was 48in long, with approximately 2in showing on each side at the bottom of the grille frame. On the 1600 Mark II model, the grille was

The shroud air vents on the 1500 and 1600, and accompanying badge on the latter model. The 1500 (white car) has an extremely rare original Mazak vent. The centre bar in particular tended to break, so the joints between this bar and the surround were beefed up on later cars – reproduction parts are always of the stronger type. On the 1600 (grey car), which has a reproduction air vent, there is an additional badge – note how the centre bar is extended beyond the numbers at either end.

substantially modified by the bars being pushed back at the bottom towards a more vertical position, and the introduction of an inner surround panel.

The chrome-plated bumpers were approximately square in section apart from a centre ridge. The top and bottom of the bumpers were flat, except that the top of the front bumper was slightly angled to let water run off. The front bumper was made out of three pieces, split behind the overriders, while the rear bumper was in one piece. Four bumper mounting points extended from the chassis through the front valance panel, carrying a black-painted bumper spring or bracket split symmetrically at the centreline of the car. The bumper was attached to the springs by three visible chrome head bolts, one in the centre and one on each corner. The overriders were mounted on black PVC mouldings and had no backing plates. They were bolted through the joined-up centre and corner sections of the bumper directly on to the bumper springs. The overriders were of a ridged design, tapering towards the bottom, and were identical front and rear. The rear bumper had only two mounting points, each supporting a bumper spring, with a total of four mounting bolts showing on the outside of the bumper. Extra distance pieces were added to the rear bumper brackets from car/chassis 102381. The front bumper had a starting handle hole in the centre towards the top. The bumpers were painted silver grey inside.

A front number plate backing plate was hung from two brackets below the front bumper. At the rear, a trapezoidal number plate mounting bracket was attached to the bumper springs, with a vertical lamp bracket which could be adjusted for height. Two different types of rear number plate backing plates were listed, one wide and shallow as normally found on home market cars, the other narrower and deeper to suit the different shape of North American number plates. It is very likely that number plate backing plates were omitted altogether on some export cars destined for markets with differently-shaped number plates.

There was next to nothing in the way of

The shroud air vents and badges on the 1600 Mark II and Twin Cam models. On this Mark II (beige car), the air vent is probably original, but is the later reinforced type. The '1600 Mk II' badge does not have the centre bar extensions. The Twin Cam (red car) has a reproduction air vent. The centre bar is not extended beyond the letters on the badge.

All models have a simple MG badge on the boot lid, with additional identifying badges on the 1600, 1600 Mark II and Twin Cam models. In all cases, these badges are the same as those found on the front shroud.

A roadster has a much flatter windscreen than a coupé. Apart from the windscreen frame itself, points to note are the additional tonneau cover fastener outboard of the grab handle on this 1600 roadster, and the wipers and washer jets.

decoration on the body, but all cars had a die-cast chrome-plated air vent on either side of the shroud towards the rear of the bonnet. The vents were oval in outline with three lateral bars, the centre one carrying the letters MGA on a grained background in a squashed octagon shape. There was a three-piece die-cast chrome-plated MG badge on the boot lid, with a thin octagonal surround and separate letters M and G, the car's body colour forming the background. The MGA 1500 had no other identification. The Twin Cam, 1600 and 1600 Mark II models had additional badges below the MG octagon on the boot lid, and behind each air vent on the front shroud. The badges were similar in design, die-cast and chrome-plated, with a grained finish centre bar carrying the letters or numbers of the respective model titles.

The windscreen was of Triplex laminated glass on all models regardless of market. The chrome-plated brass frame (made by Auster) was held in two vertical stanchions with splayed-out feet at the bottom and brackets passing through the joint of the shroud and front wings. There was a combined support and grab handle on either side, attached to the scuttle and to the stanchions. Crosshead screws were used to hold the windscreen frame to the stanchions, and the crosshead screws holding the grab handles to the stanchions were finished with domed nuts on the inside. A rubber apron provided the seal between windscreen and scuttle, and there were rubber gaskets for the stanchions where they passed through the body.

The windscreen support and grab handle. Note also the demister vent and the 'lift-the-dot' fasteners for the tonneau cover on the scuttle of this 1500 roadster.

From the front, the coupé differs from the roadster only above the waistline. The windscreen is significantly more curved in plan view. This is a 1600 model, as indicated by the combination of radiator grille and sidelamps.

From the rear, the height and curvature of the coupé roof are evident. This is the correct type of optional luggage rack, fitted in the correct manner.

COUPÉ BODY

The coupé body was of the same basic design as the roadster, but with a simple roof added. Of the major panels, the coupé front shroud was modified in the scuttle area to incorporate a lower windscreen channel, and the rear tonneau panel was cut back to the line where the lower frame of the rear screen met the panel. The windscreen was markedly more curved than on the roadster, with a chrome-plated brass finisher to the rubber surround. The wrap-around rear screen consisted of three pieces of glass, set in a rather complicated one-piece rubber surround which again had a chrome finisher. The front and rear screen chrome surround finishers were both in two pieces, with small joining clips top and bottom in the centre.

The doors were completely different, as the coupé doors had swivelling front quarterlights and wind-down windows set in thin chrome-plated brass channel surrounds. The coupé also had external door handles of a novel design. Short vertical handles protruded through oval escutcheons at the rear of the door, on the

The coupé windscreen has a sharp 'wraparound'. The rubber surround has a chrome-plated finisher like that of the rear window. The scuttle top above the facia is always trimmed on coupés, in leathercloth (Vynide) on most models but Novon plastic on the 1600 Mark II.

The coupé wing piping continues forward to the door. There is a chrome-plated finisher around the door aperture above the waistline of the car.

While the coupé rear window contains three separate pieces of glass, the rubber surround is a one-piece moulding with a two-piece chrome finisher split in the middle of the car.

Coupé window frames are made from brass and chrome-plated. The door locks are of the zero-torque type. There is only one rubber buffer on the door post and there is a finisher over the door seal along the sill.

The unusual door handle of the coupé rests on a small rubber buffer set into the window frame. Note how different the door skin is at the top compared to the roadster, and how the window frame is splayed out at the bottom rear.

rounded shoulder of the door panel just below the window. The handles were pulled down and away from the door to operate. There was a small rubber plunger on the window frame under the top of the door handle. A key-operated lock was fitted to one coupé door, originally on the left-hand door regardless of whether the car was left-hand or right-hand drive, but from 1500 coupé car/chassis 25110 this lock was fitted to the driver's door. The lock was operated by the ignition key. The other door could be locked from the inside. The actual door latches on the coupé were of the zero-torque type. Coupé doors had only one rubber buffer where roadsters had two.

The coupé door seals ran right round the door opening in one piece, being split at the front bottom corner. Retaining and protecting strips were fitted over the door seal along the sills. In addition, the coupé had rubber sealing strips on the door hinge pillars, with a separate small sealing pad above the top hinge. There was a chrome-

On a 1500 coupé, the parcel shelf is comparatively deep (top), running all the way forward to the front edge of the rear window. The parcel shelf rail is correctly in white, contrasting with the red interior trim. All 1600 and other later coupés have this shorter parcel shelf (above) with a rail which is always in the same colour as the shelf, and with fixing screws in a different position.

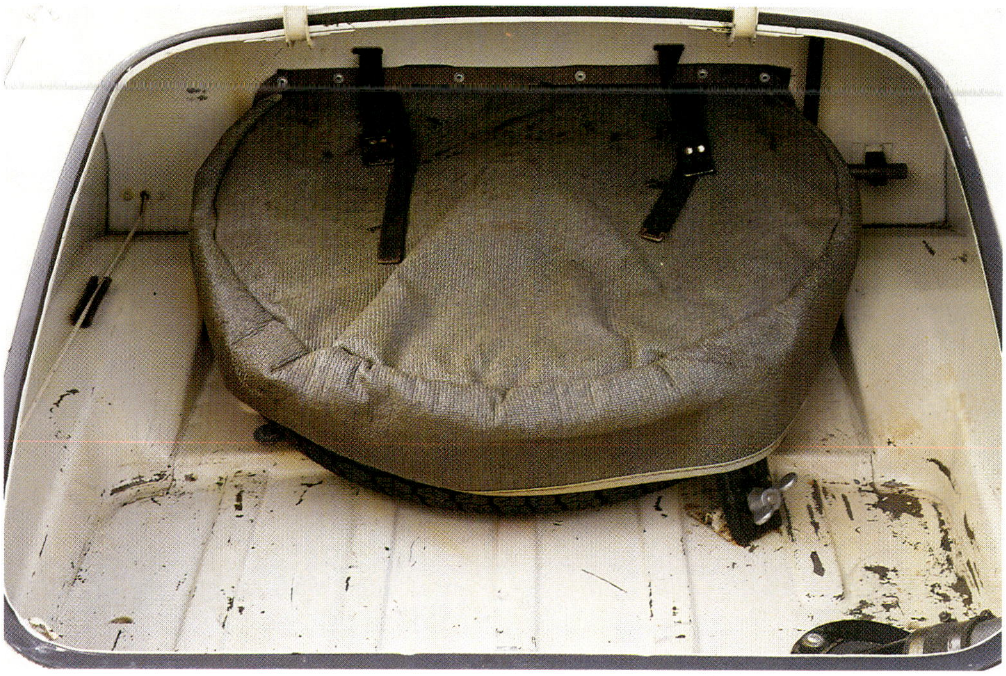

The typical MGA boot, as seen on all roadsters and early coupés. The tool bag, removed in this picture, would be held by the straps above the spare wheel cover. This cover is permanently attached to the fibreboard surround of the aperture in the rear bulkhead. The starting handle is to the right of the spare wheel, clipped to the bulkhead, and the pull rod for the boot lid release is on the left.

With the spare wheel removed and its cover lifted out of the way (below), we are looking into the carpet bag which protrudes through the bulkhead into the tonneau area behind the seats. The spare wheel rests on two felt pads, but is apt to rub and discolour the paint all the same. The spare wheel clamp is off-set to the right.

plated finisher around the upper part of the door aperture above the waistline.

An important modification occurred on the coupé body with the introduction of the 1600 model, the Twin Cam coupé being modified as well. On these later cars, the luggage space in the tonneau area behind the seats was improved by the spare wheel being relocated rearwards into the boot, and a solid rear bulkhead was introduced in place of the original type with its spare wheel aperture. This change also helped to reduce the interior noise level in the coupé – always a bit of a problem. The shelf below the rear window inside the car was cut back at the same time.

BOOT

The lack of boot space was one of the MGA's few shortcomings and was criticized even when the car was new. Soft squashable luggage would make the best of it, and the external luggage carrier was a desirable extra.

The spare wheel was mounted on the floor, protruding through an aperture in the bulkhead into the tonneau with a fibreboard surround to the aperture. The Hardura spare wheel cover was attached to this surround and was felt on the inside, grey plastic on the outside. There was a black-painted clamp on the right-hand side at the rear of the spare wheel, fastened by a wing nut on to an eye-bolt which was held captive to a cross-pin in a bracket on the boot floor. On the 1600 and Mark II coupés, as well as the later Twin Cam coupés, the spare wheel was

Spare wheel clamps: the slightly longer one (below) is the correct type for all roadsters and early coupés, while the shorter one is for 1600 and other late coupés.

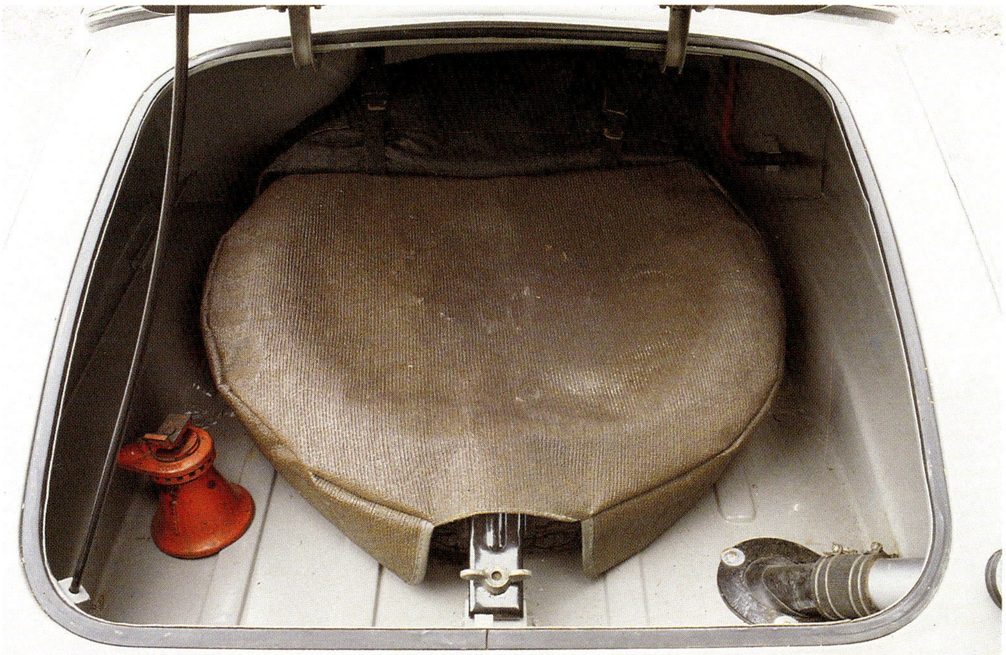

On the 1600 and later Twin Cam coupés, the spare wheel was moved rearwards to sit fully in the boot and a solid bulkhead was fitted between boot and tonneau area. The spare wheel cover is loose and the clamp is mounted centrally at the rear. Also visible are the boot prop (shaped to match the curvature of the lid), the arrangement of the fuel filler, and the sealing rubber in the channel round the boot lid aperture. In this photo the tool bag is strapped into place and the jack sits on show.

Without the spare wheel (below), the 1600 coupé's bulkhead is seen to have a central spare wheel steady bracket, and there are two support brackets for the spare wheel on the boot floor.

This squared-off style of boot floor panelwork was seen only on very early cars. This car, the fifth production MGA built and one of the original works rally cars, is fitted with the optional 20 gallon fuel tank with a filler protruding through the boot lid.

moved further back and was completely in the boot. These cars had a solid rear bulkhead with a spare wheel steady in the centre, and the clamp at the rear was centrally mounted. The spare wheel cover was loose on these later coupé models.

The starting handle was painted black, later red, and was held in three clips above and to the right of the spare wheel aperture on the bulkhead. Two straps were fixed to the bulkhead to hold the tool bag. The original tool kit was extremely comprehensive but was sadly depleted after car/chassis 93548 (MGA 1600 in 1960). Up until car/chassis 93547, as well as on all Twin Cams, MGAs were supplied with a tool roll containing the following small tools: three double-ended box spanners, three double-

This boot floor, with smoothed-off panelling, is typical of the vast majority of MGAs and was undoubtedly easier to press. Note the short piece of felt channel for the release pull rod on the highest point of the floor.

The original tool kit from a Twin Cam roadster, with the hammer for the knock-ons. This is the early complete tool kit featuring a roll of smaller tools, a tyre pump and a grease gun.

This is an original roll for the small tools from an early 1500 car on disc wheels, as demonstrated by the presence of the wheel nut spanner and the yellow tin for the Lockheed brake bleeder kit.

Two of the three jacks found in MGAs. The second type of jack (left) was the black-painted King Dick screw type with hourglass base. The final type, the orange-red Shelley with a ratchet mechanism and a round base, was supplied from July 1960.

ended open spanners, an adjustable spanner, a screwdriver for recessed head screws and an ordinary screwdriver, a pair of pliers, two tyre levers, a tyre valve spanner, a screwdriver and gauge (Lucas) for the distributor, a key to the gearbox and rear axle drain plugs, a Walters & Dobson or 'Sutty' tyre pump and a Tecalemit grease gun. Pushrod-engined cars also had a ring type spanner for tappet adjustments, a cylinder head spanner and a tappet feeler gauge (.017in on 1500 models, .015in on 1600 models). In the 1500 tool kit there was also a Lockheed brake bleeder screw and drain tube, but only early 1500 cars came with a Tipon paint touch-up pencil as standard. The Twin Cam tool kit included a .018in valve clearance gauge.

All cars were supplied with a plug spanner and tommy bar. Standard disc wheel cars were supplied with a wheel brace, while wire wheel cars, Twin Cams and De Luxe models came with a copper hammer, as well as a special octagonal spanner on those export cars which had octagonal spinners (for Germany and Switzerland). It is possible that the copper hammer was replaced by an alloy mallet from December 1961. A screw-type 6in double lift jack was supplied, worked by a separate handle. Three types or jack have been identified. Early cars had a black Shelley jack with rectangular base and a three-piece handle. The second type was a King Dick, also painted black, with hourglass-shaped base and a two-piece handle. Finally, from car/chassis 93548, came a Shelley jack with round base, a ratchet mechanism and straight single-piece handle. This jack was painted orange-red. For the later cars, a dealer-supplied additional tool kit was available (see section on options, extras and accessories).

The standard roadster seats as found on all models, here in black and therefore with correct contrast colour piping. The centre armrest features similar piping. The pull cable for the door lock can be seen inside the door pocket.

With trim in other colours than black, piping is in the main trim colour. The metal strip along the lower edge of the door pocket shows up well here.

Roadster Interior Trim

The standard roadster seats were asymmetrical in design in that the seat squabs were slightly higher towards the centre line of the car. The squabs had six pleats with markedly wider border panels, while the seat cushions were slightly narrower and so had in effect eight pleats of the same width. The seat backs were hinged and folded forward for access to the tonneau area. The cushions lifted out to reveal black-painted tubular seat frames. The cushion bases were plywood with a central wire mesh insert, covered with Dunlopillo foam rubber. The squabs were padded with Hairlok rubberized hair.

The actual upholstery of cushions and squabs was leather on the wearing parts, Vynide leathercloth (ICI quality TXL.1A) on the edges and on the back of the squabs. Seat edge piping was in contrast colours on black seats, and in the main seat colour on seats of other colours (please refer to the colour scheme tables found later in this book). Both seats had longitudinal adjustment on the seat slides, with the release lever on the outside slide. There were no changes to the roadster seats during production, apart from the revised colours introduced at the

The de-luxe (or competition) seats have additional piping around the centre panels, again in contrast colour on black seats. These particular seats have been restored with modern seat foams which give a rather too pronounced curvature to the edge bolsters. Among other options, this car features the ashtray in the correct position in front of the armrest.

On this Twin Cam roadster, the de-luxe seats are all original, and show the typical sagging of the original Dunlopillo foam after 30-plus years.

start of 1600 production. While it seems that 1500 roadster seats were upholstered in Connolly's Celstra leather, the differently grained and slightly better quality Vaumol leather, also by Connolly, was apparently introduced on the 1600 and later models.

The door casings were in hardboard, the door pockets and other interior casings in millboard, including the scuttle side casings in the footwells (with small infill pieces covering the body mountings) and the rear quarter casings. All were covered in Vynide leathercloth (ICI quality TXL.1B) matching the seat colour. The casings were affixed with self-tapping crosshead screws, chrome-plated with chrome-plated cup washers. The door pocket aperture had rounded corners and a metal strip along its lower edge, painted to match the trim colour. The door locks were activated by pull cords covered in black plastic inside the door pockets.

The carpet was Crossley's Karvel, normally black on roadsters except possibly on very early 1500 models, which may have had carpet to tone with the interior trim colour. The floor, gearbox and propeller shaft

With a seat cushion removed, the seat frames and slides can be seen, together with the handbrake (always on the right-hand side of the tunnel), here in the off position. The carpet shown here is the original Karvel, with edge binding only at the rear edges of the front and middle sections of the tunnel carpet.

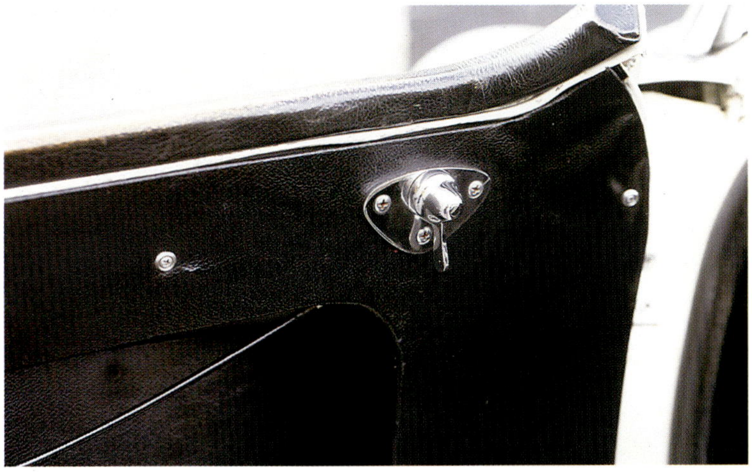

On the 1500 model as well as early Twin Cam roadsters, the front sidescreen was held tight by this half-wing nut.

This knurled nut for the front sidescreen fixing was introduced from the start of the 1600 model.

The roadster door trim is simplicity itself. Note the position of the fixing screws, the metal edge to the door pocket and the pull cord for the door lock inside the pocket, together with the door lock itself.

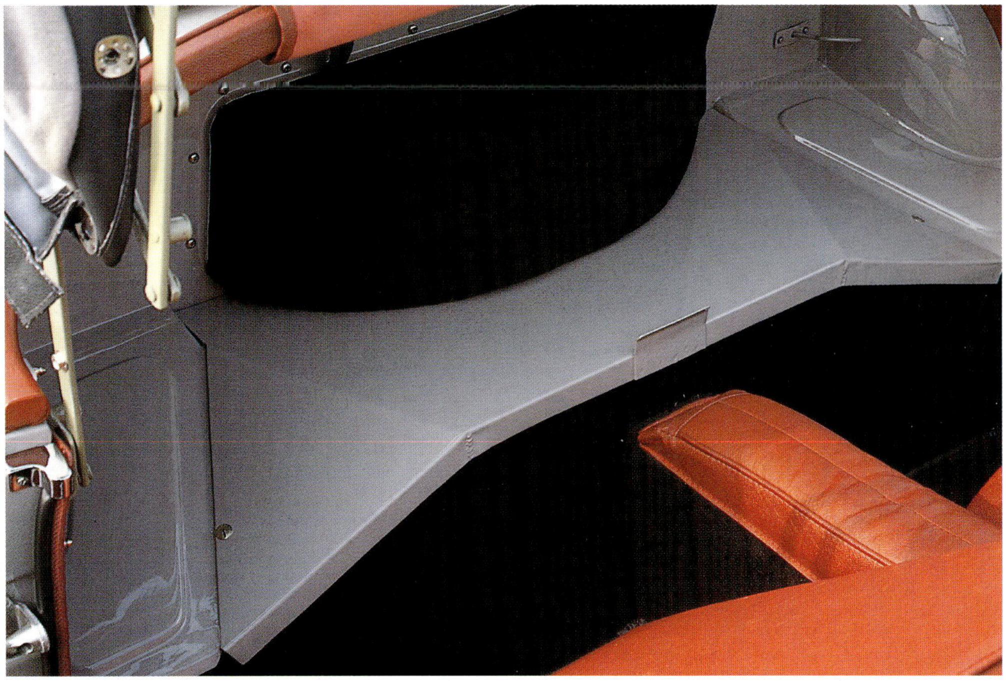

The correct appearance of the tonneau area on the roadster, with no carpeting over the removable battery hatch, but carpet on the heelboard and for the spare wheel bag. Note the small plate at the centre front of the battery hatch, found on later 1600 roadsters to help keep the sidescreen envelope in place.

Although an exact change point is unknown, it was probably in mid-1956 when the original all-wood trim roll bases for door tops and rear quarters were changed. The new door top pieces incorporated cast aluminium front and rear sections.

tunnels and the heelboard behind the seats were all carpeted. The floor of the hood stowage compartment, including the battery access hatch, was not carpeted, nor were the rear wheelarches or the rear bulkhead. The spare wheel bag attached to the rear bulkhead was in carpet. The carpet was not edge-bound, except for the cut-outs around the chassis crossmember in front of the seats, the rear edges of the front and intermediate tunnel carpets, and the edges of the flap over the gearbox dipstick cover. The floor and toeboard carpets were held in place by lift-the-dot fasteners, other carpets were glued, while the gearbox dipstick flap was held in place by one durable dot press stud fastener. There was felt underlay only under the front floor carpet, and the tunnel carpets including the gearbox dipstick cover flap. The sills and the chassis crossmember in front of the seats were also covered in carpet, glued in place. The rear tunnel carpet incorporated a centre armrest with a Dunlopillo base, upholstered in leather in two pleats for the top and Vynide leathercloth for the borders. The armrest had piping around the edge of the top, and the colour of armrest and piping matched the seat colour and seat piping colour respectively. A rubber heelmat was set into the carpet in the driver's footwell.

The cockpit edges were finished off with trim rolls, on wood or cast aluminium bases. Until mid-1956, the door trim rolls and rear quarter pieces had all-wood bases, but on later cars cast aluminium was used for the rear quarters and for the front end of the door trim rolls. The trim rolls on the door tops and the small curved rear quarter pieces were covered in leather, while the trim rolls across the top of the facia and the central piece across the front edge of the rear tonneau panel were covered in Vynide leathercloth (quality TXL.1B). Each trim roll had piping towards the outside of the car. The colour of the trim roll covers and of the piping matched the colours of the seats and seat piping respectively. The facia trim roll was padded with a thin layer of soft rubber between the wood base and the Vynide cover.

Available as an optional extra were the competition de-luxe seats, which were introduced in September 1958 at the time the Twin Cam model appeared. They were most commonly fitted on the Twin Cam but also became available on pushrod-engined cars at the same time. They were rather different in construction from the standard seats in that the cushions did not lift out but were integral with the seat frames. Being wider than the standard seats, they had seat slides set further apart, so the floorboards were modified and different screws were used for fitting the slides. The competition de-luxe seats had horseshoe-shaped borders to both squab and cushion, the central area of each being divided into five pleats. There was piping to the edge of the seats and around the central areas. As on the standard seats, the piping was in a contrast colour on black seats, and in the main seat colour on other seats. The upholstery was probably always in Vaumol leather on these seats. Apart from the change in the colour range which occurred from the start of 1600 production and simultaneously on the Twin Cam, the competition de-luxe seats were not altered during the production run. Exactly the same seats could be supplied on the coupé models.

These are the standard coupé seats with transverse pleating – all original and with a nice patina.

Coupé Interior Trim

The seats fitted as standard on coupé models were of a similar construction to those of the roadster, but differed in their trim pattern. The squabs had a border panel each side with four transverse pleats in the centre, and rather deeper top and bottom panels. This motif was repeated on the cushions, but without

This is the more elaborate coupé door trim. Although shown on a 1600 Mark II model, these trim panels were not changed during coupé production.

The battery hatch is carpeted on the coupé. This car, an early Twin Cam coupé, is fitted with de-luxe seats, the same as those available on the roadster. Note that the tunnel armrest on the coupé is plain, without the pleats of the roadster armrest.

A detail showing the deep shelf on the original 1500-type coupé body, with the protruding spare wheel below.

the border panels, so the cushion pleats ran right across the seat cushions. It is thought that coupé seats were upholstered in Vaumol leather from the start of production in 1956. They had edge piping, and the seat colours and piping colours were the same as found on the roadster models. The centre armrest was not pleated on coupés.

The coupé trim was generally more elaborate than on the roadster. This was particularly true of the 1500 and early Twin Cam coupés, which sometimes had two-tone colour schemes for the leathercloth trim. On the 1600 and later Twin Cam coupés the colour schemes were rationalized, so that single-colour trim was then found on all coupés (please refer to the tables of colour schemes found later in this book).

Because of the coupé's wind-down windows, the door casings were completely different and had no map pockets. Each door casing had a centre panel with four horizontal pleats, surrounded by piping. The door capping was a separate piece, sometimes in a contrast colour. Each door was fitted with a door pull with Bakelite handgrip of a type also seen on some BMC saloon cars. Similarly, the chrome-plated interior door handles and window winder handles were of standardized Nuffield/BMC types.

In order to replace the lost door pockets, there was a map pocket on the scuttle side casing on each side, lined in off-white material similar to the headlining. There was a trim roll across the top of the facia. The rear quarter casings had separate cappings which were originally colour-coded to the trim, but which became uniformly off-white for all colour schemes on 1600 and later models (although some experts believe these cappings were still colour-coded on the later coupés). Across the base of the rear window was a ledge which was actually referred to as a parcel shelf (some joke, surely), with a separate finisher rail on the front edge. These parts could again be in contrast colours on the 1500 models. On the 1600 models, the parcel shelf was cut back to allow easier access to the tonneau area, and the shelf and the rail were both in the main trim colour.

In addition to those areas which were carpeted on the roadster, the coupé also had carpeting to the floor of the tonneau compartment, including the battery hatch, rear wheelarches and rear bulkhead – but

Behind the seats on a 1600 coupé, showing the solid carpet-covered bulkhead and the short shelf. Not all of the carpeting seen here is original.

there was no additional underfelt. The floor and tunnel carpets were similar to those of the roadster. The carpet quality was the same but the normal colour on the coupé was light grey, except on a few early cars which had black carpets or cars supplied to special order with this carpet colour. On the 1500 and early Twin Cam coupés, the spare wheel protruded into the tonneau area, and was covered in a grey carpet bag. On the 1600 and later Twin Cam coupé, the spare wheel was relocated rearwards completely into the boot, and a solid rear bulkhead completely covered in carpet was introduced.

The coupé headlining was mounted on three bows and was in an off-white plastic material on all cars. Similarly, off-white trim pieces were used on the cant rails surrounding the top frames of the doors, the header rail above the windscreen and below the rear window, while the windscreen pillars were covered in the same material.

The facia and scuttle top were always covered in Vynide leathercloth on the coupé models (see the section on facia and instruments). Sound deadening foam rubber was fitted to the underside of the scuttle. This may have been available to special order also on roadsters. As mentioned above, the coupé models could also be supplied with the competition de-luxe seats, of the same type as found on the roadster.

If no specific difference between roadster and coupé trim has been mentioned in this section, it may be assumed that the trim was identical for the two body styles.

A cut-off section of the original one-piece door seal, which is now difficult to find.

WEATHER EQUIPMENT

The three-bow hood frame with a wooden front hoodstick was permanently attached to the rear quarter side casings behind the doors. The frame was normally painted tan, but replacement hood frames were black. An unspecified change to the hood frame occurred very early in the 1500 production run, at car/chassis 10501. From 1600 car/chassis 78249 and Twin Cam 2540, there were extensive changes to the hood frame, canopy and other parts, to enable the hood to stow more compactly under the rear tonneau panel and to improve rearwards seat adjustment.

The hood canopy was from ICI Vynide material, in black or ice blue, on the 1500 models and the early Twin Cams. The canopy was changed at car/chassis 10501

The general style of hood is similar on most MGA cars, but the black hood colour was found only on 1500 models and early Twin Cams. The flap-type sidescreen, with a spring-loaded closing device at the front, is also found only on these models.

Hood quarterlights were introduced in September 1956 after the first 10,000 cars had been built. Hoods without quarterlights are now hardly, if ever, seen. This illustration also shows the hood fasteners on the rear tonneau panel.

A 1500 type sidescreen showing the flap in the open position. The hood valance around the sidescreen should be compared with the later photo of a 1600 hood.

The additional over-centre catch fitted to the front hood stick from the introduction of the 1600 model.

The inside of the 1500 hood, with all three hood bows covered in fabric. The chrome wing bolt for fastening the hood on to one of the windscreen frame pegs can also be seen.

(see above), and again at car/chassis 20162 when the original single rear window was supplemented by quarterlight panels. Both these and the rear window were in Vybak material. A change not recorded in the parts list occurred at car/chassis 16101 when the hood seams were capped and welded after stitching to improve the weatherproofing.

With the introduction of the 1600 model from car/chassis 68851, the hood material was changed to Wardle's Everflex, in grey, blue or beige, always with tan backing material. The new hood canopies were found on the Twin Cam from car/chassis 2193. The canopy was modified at car/chassis 78249 together with the frame. The final change to the hood canopy was at car/chassis 96269, when the hood valance was modified to suit altered sidescreens which were introduced to improve weatherproofing.

Two pegs on the windscreen frame fitted into sockets in the front hoodstick, which was then held tight by two wing bolts. From the start of 1600 production, and on the Twin Cam from car/chassis 2193, an additional over-centre catch was fitted to the centre of the front hoodstick and the windscreen frame. At the rear, a metal attachment strip slid into a channel on the rear edge of the hood canopy, anchoring the hood to two chrome-plated hood retaining plates on the tonneau panel. In addition there were three lift-the-dot fasteners on each side of the tonneau panel and a turn-button fastener on each rear quarter portion of the cockpit trim roll. On the inside, a press stud on a short strap each side fastened the canopy to the hood frame.

The standard type of sidescreen on the 1500 models and early Twin Cams was of the flap type, with the lower part of each sidescreen being a signalling flap held in place by a spring-loaded closing device. The flaps also served to give access to the door release pulls when the hood and sidescreens were erected. The sidescreen frames were covered in Vynide matching the hood colour. Sidescreens were held in place by two tan-painted brackets, the rearmost with a peg fitting into a socket with a chrome-plated bezel on the door trim roll, the front one attaching to a stud on the inside door trim. The stud was mounted on a rounded triangular backing plate and had a half-wing or lever tightening nut with a domed head. The 1500 sidescreens were changed at car/chassis 10501, together with the hood frame and hood canopy. Some sidescreens had a small metal tab at the front edge catching behind the windscreen when the door closed, to prevent the sidescreen moving outwards at speed.

On the 1600 model, and on the Twin Cam from car/chassis 2193, sidescreens were changed to the sliding type, with a two-part perspex window. The front half was fixed, but the rear half slid forward inside the front half and was fitted with two perspex blocks for finger purchase, on the outside at the rear and on the inside at the front. Sidescreen frames were still covered in hood-type material, now grey, beige or blue. Another

The beige colour was one of three used for the Everflex hoods found from the start of 1600 production, as well as on the later Twin Cams. Simultaneously, the sliding sidescreens, with frames covered in hood material, were introduced.

On the later 1600-type hood, the transverse hood bows were left bare but the front bow ran in a channel sewn into the hood cover.

The hood colour on this 1600 roadster is grey. This hood has the later type of valance round the sidescreen – compare with the similar photo of the 1500 hood.

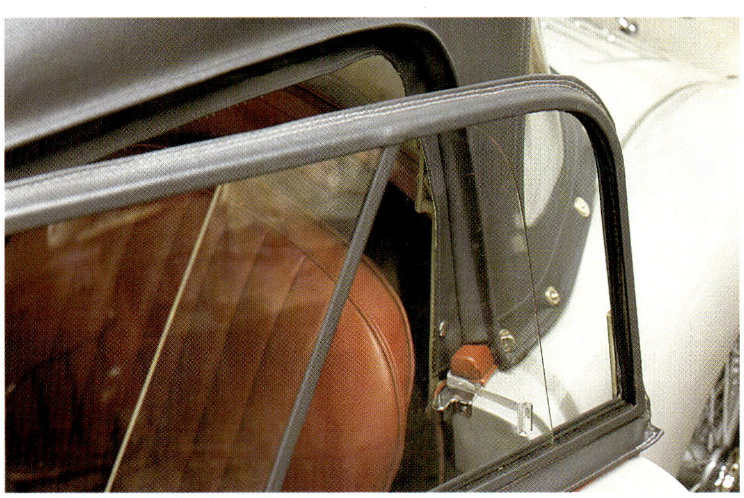

This 1600 Mark II De Luxe model is fitted with the aluminium-framed sliding sidescreens. They were recommended for use if a hard top was fitted.

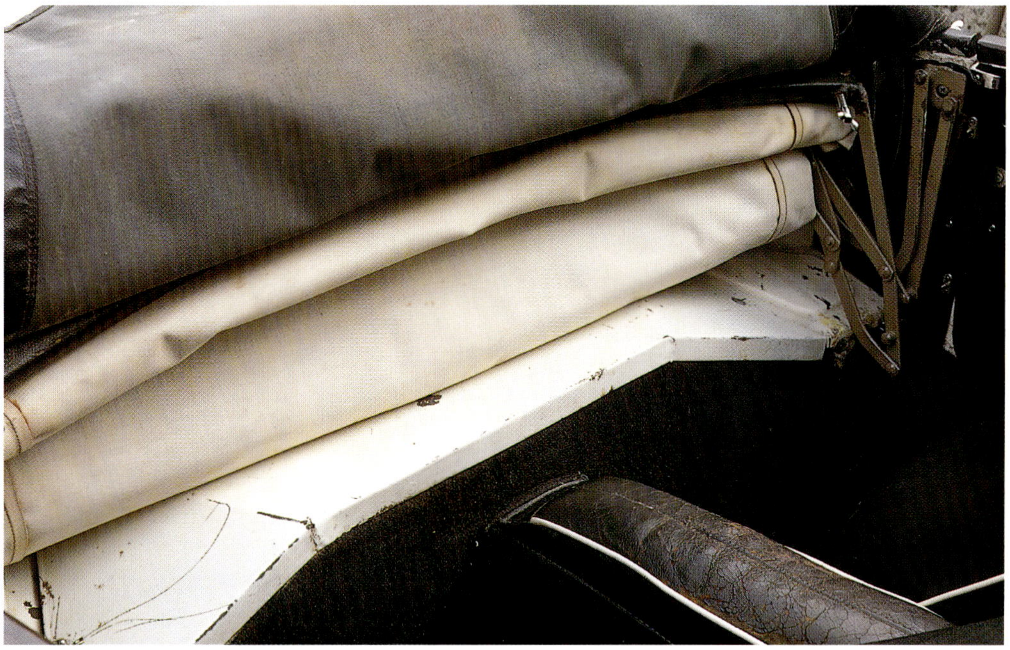

On both of these cars (left and below) the hoods have been rather casually folded. Greater care should be taken with the hood fabric to avoid getting it trapped between the hood sticks, damaging the rear window and quarterlights. The car with black trim is a 1500, the one with red trim a 1600 Mark II. The point is to show how the final type of hood frame was stowed further back under the tonneau panel – note the difference in the angle between the scissor legs of the hood frame to the right in both pictures.

change introduced at the start of 1600 production, and correspondingly on the Twin Cam, was that the front sidescreen fixing stud on the inside door casing was given a round knurled dome nut. The flap on the rear edge of the sidescreens was deleted from car/chassis 96269 (or slightly later depending on sidescreen colour, as outlined in the list of change points) with the hood canopy being modified to suit. The standard sidescreens and hoods were made by the Coventry Hood and Sidescreen Company.

Available as an optional extra, and always supplied if the hard top was fitted, were aluminium sliding sidescreens made by Weathershields. There were two different types, one for the original aluminium hard top, the other for the later fibreglass hard top.

All cars had a sidescreen stowage envelope hung in the tonneau area behind the seats, consisting of a metal frame covered in TXL.1A leathercloth which was always coloured to match the trim. It was fixed with three lift-the-dot fasteners to each rear quarter casing, with the flap of the envelope held in place by a single central lift-the-dot. The sidescreen stowage envelope was modified at car/chassis 78249 (1600) or 2540 (Twin Cam) to fit above rather than in front of the battery access hatch, thus giving more rearwards seat adjustment. The envelope was rather inconvenient in that the hood was stowed behind it, so it had to be removed whenever one wanted to raise or lower the hood. Probably for this reason it is now frequently not fitted.

The original type of sidescreen envelope and battery hatch (below), here in the rare 1500 colour of Glacier Blue, and the later type of sidescreen envelope and battery hatch introduced in October 1959 (above).

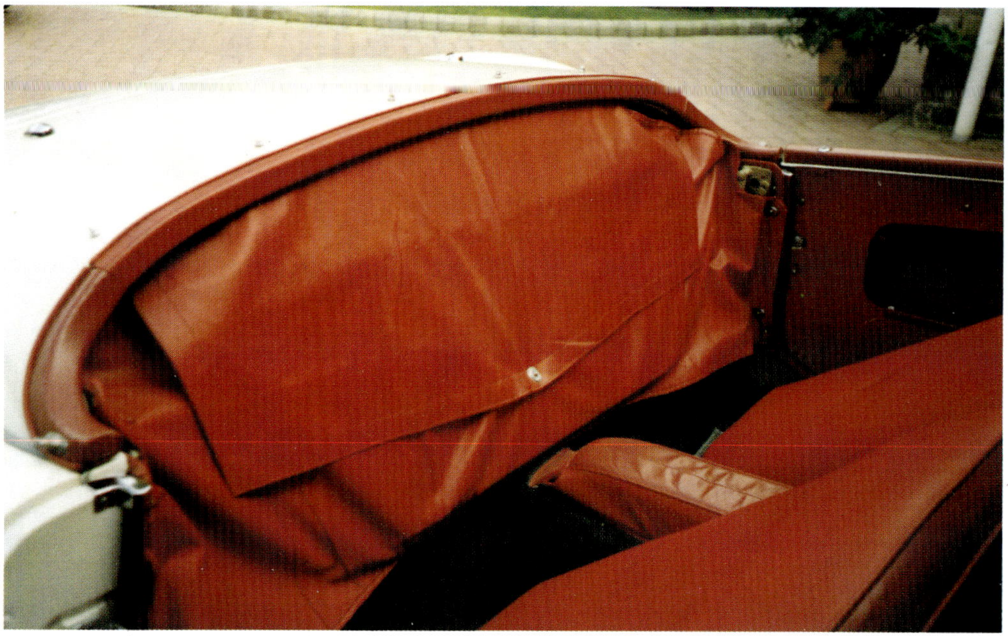

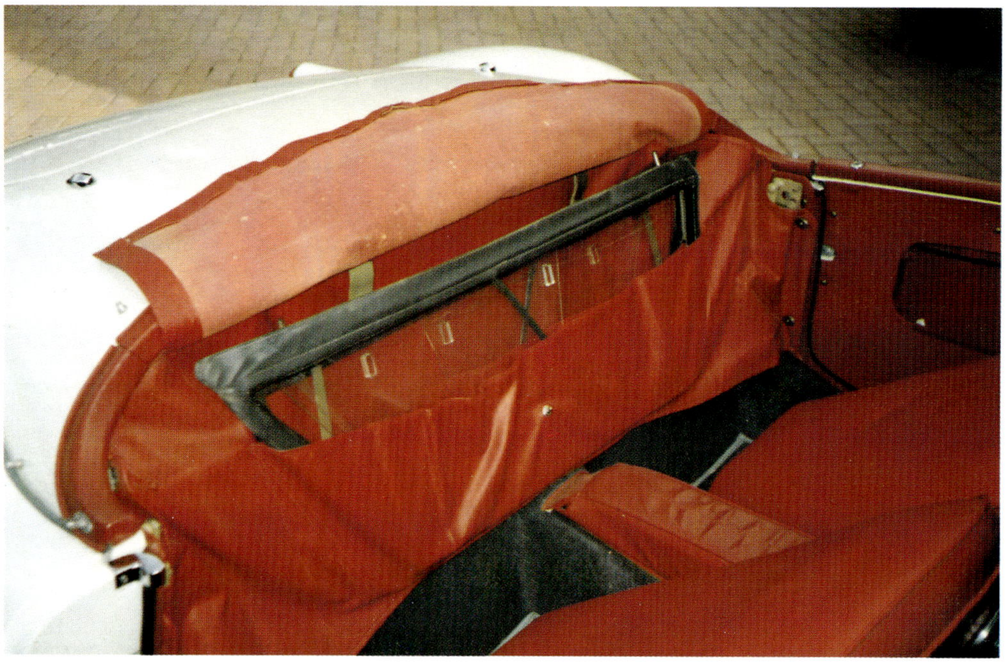

The sidescreen envelope hangs from the underside of the rear tonneau panel and is attached with three lift-the-dot fasteners to each rear quarter casing. A single lift-the-dot holds down the flap covering the storage pocket. The lower photograph shows the correct way to store the sidescreens.

The tonneau cover was an optional extra on all cars, and was supplied in the same material and colour as the hood, except that 1500 models painted Black, Tyrolite Green or Glacier Blue could have the combination of an ice blue hood and black tonneau cover. The tonneau cover had a zip fastener offset to the passenger side. It was secured by six lift-the-dot fasteners at the front of the rear tonneau panel, to the hood turn-button fasteners, by four lift-the-dot fasteners to each door top, and by six lift-the-dot fasteners on the scuttle, three on each side between mirror and grab handle. From car/chassis 60637 (left-hand drive 1500 models), 64332 (right-hand drive 1500 models) and Twin Cam 994, the fasteners on the door tops were discontinued as was the steering wheel bag, and the tonneau cover zip was lengthened. The scuttle lift-the-dots were relocated so there was one on each side of the mirror, and one on each side of each grab handle. The colours were changed from the start of the 1600 model and on the Twin Cam at the same time.

Facia & Instruments

The facia panels on roadsters and coupés were different pressings, with round-the-

The original type 1500 tonneau cover, here on a left-hand drive car, was fixed to four lift-the-dot fasteners on each door top, as well as fasteners on the rear tonneau panel and the scuttle. This style of tonneau cover had a sewn-in steering wheel bag.

In late 1958 or early 1959, a revised tonneau cover without a steering wheel bag was introduced, and the fasteners on the door tops were deleted. The fasteners on the rear tonneau panel were the same but the disposition of those on the scuttle was changed. Note how this style of tonneau cover has a much more pronounced ear in the front corner, as the fastener in this corner is now on the scuttle rather than on the door. This is the grey colour found on the weather equipment of 1600 and other late models.

corner end pieces added on coupé facias, but the layout of the instruments and controls was exactly the same on all models. The panel was painted on 1500 and 1600 roadsters, usually to match the exterior colour, except on black cars where the panel was painted to match the trim colour. On Twin Cam and 1600 Mark II roadsters, the panel was covered in Vynide leathercloth to match the trim colour. On all roadsters, the facia trim roll was the same colour as the other trim rolls and the trim in general. The 1500, 1600 and Twin Cam roadsters had the scuttle top painted body colour, but on 1600 Mark II roadsters it was covered in Novon plastic material in either red or black. Twin Cam and 1600 Mark II roadsters had a stainless steel finishing strip to the lower edge of their leathercloth-covered facia panels.

All coupés had the facia covered in leathercloth, with a stainless steel finisher to the lower edge. On 1500 and early Twin Cam coupés, the facia and scuttle top could be in two different colours of leathercloth, one of which matched the seat colour, while the facia trim roll would match either the facia or the scuttle top. On 1600 and later Twin Cam coupés, the facia, scuttle top and facia trim roll were all the same colour, matching the seat colour. On 1600 Mark II

There are only detail differences between the facia panels of the various MGA models. On this left-hand drive 1500 roadster, it should be noted that the relative positions of the instruments are the same as on the right-hand drive cars: rev counter on the left and speedometer on the right, fuel gauge to the left of the radio speaker grille and dual gauge to the right. The white Tudor windscreen washer push is one of several types that may correctly be found on the MGA.

This right-hand drive 1600 roadster lacks a washer. The awkward position for the indicator warning lamp on the extreme right may just be seen – it is usually hidden behind the rim of the steering wheel.

The extras fitted on this 1600 Mark I De Luxe model include one of several different period radios, a windscreen washer with another type of knob and the wood rim steering wheel.

On the Twin Cam roadster, the facia panel is covered in Vynide but the scuttle top above the facia is still painted body colour. Note also the bright frame around the speaker grille and the finisher along the lower edge of the panel. This car is interesting because it is not fitted with a heater.

On the 1600 Mark II roadster, the facia was effectively changed to the Twin Cam type, with Vynide covering and a chrome-plated bezel for the loudspeaker grille – but the covered scuttle was unique to this model among roadsters. This left-hand drive De Luxe model is fitted with tonneau cover fittings on the scuttle of the correct lay-out for the 1500 model, but wrong for this car.

Similarities are even closer between the different coupé facias, which were always covered in Vynide, together with the scuttle panels. The Twin Cam style radio speaker grille frame and the lower edge panel finisher are common to all coupés. This is a 1600 model.

This is an early Twin Cam with the 1500-style body, but you would not know it from the facia, except from the Twin Cam rev counter. This car has the period push-button type of radio and is fitted with the headlamp flasher activated by the stalk type switch visible through the steering wheel. The way in which the ends of the facia differ in shape on a coupé is worth noting.

coupés, the leathercloth on the scuttle top was replaced by Novon in either red or black. All cars had coloured plastic piping at the top edge of the facia panel, below the trim roll ('facia piping'), and also behind the trim roll butting up to the scuttle panel ('facia trim roll piping'). The facia piping was a fatter section than the trim roll piping.

The instrument and control layout on left-hand drive cars was generally a mirror image of that found on right-hand drive cars, except that the relative positions of the instruments were not changed. On all cars, therefore, the rev counter was on the left and the speedometer on the right, with the fuel gauge to the left of the radio speaker grille and the dual oil/water gauge to the right. The layout is as follows, starting from the *right* on a right-hand drive car and from the *left* on a left-hand drive car:

Indicator warning light (Lucas WL13, green glass, chrome-plated bezel)
Indicator switch (Lucas TPS1, self-cancelling air valve type)
Headlamp flasher switch (optional extra, Lucas 23SA)
Speedometer on right-hand drive cars; rev counter on left-hand drive cars
Panel light switch marked P with arrow (Lucas CHR1 or 3R, rheostat dimming)
Rev counter on right-hand drive cars; speedometer on left-hand drive cars
Fog lamp switch marked F (Lucas PS7), wired on all cars regardless of whether fog lamp(s) fitted
Oil/water gauge on right-hand drive cars; fuel gauge on left-hand drive cars
Above: light switch marked L (Lucas PPG1, pull and twist/pull)
Below: starter pull marked S (not on cars with steering lock)
Above: radio loudspeaker grille
Centre: horn push (Lucas HP19)
Below: heater controls (optional extra)
Above: ignition lock (Lucas S45; Wilmot Breeden FA or FP series key), but not on cars with steering lock
Below: choke pull marked C
Fuel gauge on right-hand drive cars; oil/water gauge on left-hand drive cars
Above: wiper switch marked W (Lucas PS7)
Below: windscreen washer marked Push (optional extra, Tudor)
Cigar lighter (optional extra, Casco Tex)
Radio aperture blanking plate or radio
Map light with chrome-plated cover (Lucas 534)
Map light switch not marked (Lucas PS7)

Three styles of speedometer: the original type (left), the later speedometer which looks similar on all models (centre), and an example of the kilometres speedometer (right). While the kph speedometer conforms to the style found on most MGAs, this particular instrument's Smiths code number indicates that it actually belongs to an early MGB (see speedometer table).

Three types of rev counter: the original style (left), the later version common to all pushrod models (centre), and the Twin Cam type with a higher rev limit (right).

MGA SPEEDOMETERS

BMC number	Smiths number	Description (application, mph/kph, rear axle ratio)
?	?	Early 1500 (to 14089), mph, 4.555:1
AHH 5184	51-116-104-01 SN.6104/01	Early 1500 (to 14089), kph, 4.555:1
AHH 5185	51-116-104-02 SN.6104/02	Early 1500 (to 14089), mph, 4.3:1
AHH 5186	51-116-104-03 SN.6104/03	Early 1500 (to 14089), kph, 4.3:1
17H 292	SN.6104/06 SN.6161/06	1500/1600/Twin Cam, mph, 4.3:1
17H 293	SN.6104/07 SN.6161/07	1500/1600/Twin Cam, kph, 4.3:1
17H 294	SN.6104/08 SN.6161/08	1500/1600/Twin Cam, mph, 4.3:1, accurate for police use
17H 295	SN.6104/09 SN.6104/17 SN.6161/17	1500/1600/Twin Cam, mph, 4.555:1
17H 296	SN.6104/10 SN.6104/18 SN.6161/18	1500/1600/Twin Cam, kph, 4.555:1
17H 297	SN.6104/11 SN.6161/20	1500/1600/Twin Cam, mph, 4.555:1, accurate for police use
BHA 4060	SN.6104/12 SN.6161/12	1500/1600/Twin Cam and 1600 Mark II, mph, 4.1:1
BHA 4061	SN.6104/13 SN.6161/13	1500/1600/Twin Cam and 1600 Mark II, kph, 4.1:1
BHA 4062	SN.6104/14 (SN.6161/14?)	1500/1600/Twin Cam and 1600 Mark II, mph, 4.1:1, accurate for police use
BHA 4068	SN.6104/15 SN.6161/15	all models, mph, 3.909:1 (competition use)
BHA 4069	SN.6104/16 SN.6161/16	all models, kph, 3.909:1 (competition use)
BHA 4128	SN.6161/25	Twin Cam, mph, 4.875:1 (competition use)
BHA 4129	SN.6161/26	Twin Cam, kph, 4.875:1 (competition use)
BHA 4145	SN.6161/21	1600 (from June 1959), mph, 4.3:1, accurate for police use
BHA 4220	SN.6161/30	1600 Mark II, mph, 4.555:1
BHA 4221	SN.6161/31	1600 Mark II, kph, 4.555:1
BHA 4222	SN.6161/32	1600 Mark II, kph, 4.555:1, blue main beam warning light
BHA 4226	SN.6161/33	1600 Mark II, kph, 4.1:1, blue main beam warning light
BHA 4227	SN.6161/22	1600 Mark II, mph, 4.1:1, accurate for police use

Notes: The change in the Smiths numbers from 6104 to 6161 which occurred in September 1958 refers to a very slight change in internal speedometer gearing in terms of revs per mile. There was no speedometer available to suit the rear axle ratio of 5.125:1 which was offered on the Twin Cam for competition use.

The left-hand pair of gauges are of the original 1500 style, while the right-hand pair are the more common type introduced in 1956. An illustration of a Centigrade water temperature gauge appears in the section dealing with export variations found later in this book.

All controls and switches were black (except the white windscreen washer push) and fitted with round knobs (except the lever-type indicator switch), with white letters where engraved. They had round chrome-plated bezels.

The speedometer incorporated a three-figure plus decimal trip mileage recorder and a five-figure total mileage recorder, with a red headlamp main beam warning light at the bottom of the dial. On some late 1600 Mark II cars with kilometres speedometers, the main beam warning light became blue. The rev counter had a red ignition and charging warning light at the bottom of the dial. The instruments were made by Smiths but were marked British Jaeger.

The original 1500 model had rather stylized instrument typography with somewhat inadequate markings. From car/chassis 14090, simpler typography with ladder scales and more frequent markings was introduced, and found on all models thereafter. The original speedometer was marked 10/30/50 etc up to 110mph, the later speedometers were marked 0/10/20 etc up to 120mph. Kilometres speedometers were marked up to 200kph. The accompanying table lists the 23 different speedometers known to have been used on various MGA models – it is hopefully reasonably complete. The Smiths numbers are marked on the dials.

Rev counters are easier to deal with because there were only three types. The original 1500 rev counter (BMC part number AHH 5187, Smiths number RN.51-112-00) was marked 5/15/25 etc up to 65, with an amber sector from 5500rpm and a red sector from 6000rpm. On 1500 models from car/chassis 14090, and on all 1600 and 1600 Mark II models, the rev counter was marked 0/5/10 etc up to 70, with amber and red sectors as before (BMC part number 17H300, Smiths number RN.2300/01 or later RN.2350/01). The Twin Cam rev counter was similar but went up to 75, with the amber sector from 6500rpm and the red sector from 7000rpm (BMC part number BHA 4083, Smiths number RN.2300/02). All rev counters were driven mechanically, from the rear end of the camshaft on pushrod-engined cars or the half-speed shaft on the Twin Cam.

The typography of the smaller gauges was changed at car/chassis 14090 in line with the bigger instruments, but there were no other changes. The fuel gauges were always marked E-$^1/_2$-F. The original fuel gauge was BMC part number AHH 5189, Smiths number FG.2530/25; the later fuel gauge was BMC part number 17H 299, Smiths number FG.2530/05. The original oil pressure gauge was marked 0-25-50-75-100, the later type 0-20-40-60-80-100. The original water temperature gauge registered in degrees Fahrenheit and was marked 90-160-190-230, the later type 90-120-160-190-212-230. From 1500 car/ chassis 57574 a water temperature gauge registering in degrees Centigrade (Celsius) was made available on left-hand drive cars, and from February 1961 this was standardized on all export cars with kilometres speedometers. The first type dual oil/water gauge was BMC part number AHH 5188, Smiths number GD.1501/00. The later type was BMC part number 17H 298, Smiths number GD.1501/01. The Centigrade gauge was BMC part number BHA 4110, Smiths number GD.1501/04.

All instruments had black dials with white figures and markings. Pointers were white, with chrome-finish centres for the speedometer and rev counter needles. The instruments were individually rim-lit, and were mounted in chrome-plated bezels.

The radio loudspeaker grille was bright anodized aluminium and was fitted from the back of the facia panel. On cars with leathercloth-covered facias (all coupés, Twin Cam roadsters and 1600 Mark II roadsters) there was a rectangular chrome bezel surrounding the grille and the horn push, completely filling the centre section of the panel. The radio aperture blanking panel was fitted in a chrome-plated bezel, and carried a chrome MG badge. The panel was painted or covered in leathercloth to match the main facia panel.

The heater controls (where fitted) were found on a small black add-on panel below the centre of the main facia, and consisted of two round black knobs, one on either side, each with two concentric rings, and a sliding knob marked B in the centre. The panel was marked as follows: left-hand side, 'Push' above and 'Air' below knob; right-hand side, 'Pull to increase' above and 'Demist' below knob; centre below slide, 'Min Temperature Max'. The sliding knob pulled out to activate the blower fan.

On the scuttle top above the facia were two chrome-plated demister vents, and in the centre the rear view mirror on a chrome-plated stalk fixed to the scuttle with two crosshead screws. The mirror backing plate was painted metallic tan or gold. Some cars exported to France had a special framed mirror, but most mirrors were unframed.

On the late Mark II export cars fitted with a steering lock, the redundant holes for the ignition lock and the starter pull were filled with special blanking buttons. Generally on 1600 Mark II models, the direction indicator warning light was moved inboard and upwards of the switch to be more clearly seen through the steering wheel, and the dimple for the warning light in the panel was omitted. Some late US export cars may have lacked the warning light altogether.

MGAs for the home market (and some export cars) were supplied with a licence holder on the windscreen. This had a chrome-plated metal backing plate on the roadster, later superseded by a plastic type which was found on all coupés. The final touch as far as originality is concerned: each MGA was supplied with a leather key fob, the colour of which matched the leather on the seats. It was printed with the MG logo on one side. The extra ignition key supplied with each car was screwed to the horizontal shelf behind the engine, in front of the heater.

PUSHROD ENGINE

The BMC B-series engine was based on the original Austin A40 engine of 1200cc introduced in 1947, but the 1.5-litre version was much changed when it appeared in 1953. This first B-series engine had a

This left-hand drive 1500 engine bay shows the dynamo-mounted ignition coil of this model, as well as the flasher relay on the bulkhead behind the heater. The windscreen washer bottle is of the early type with the narrow neck

On the normal 1600 model, the ignition coil has disappeared from sight, down to a bracket on the engine mounting. There are a few incorrect details: the nuts and bolts for the cylinder head and rocker cover should be painted, while the plate on the radiator should be out of sight on the back of the header tank. The plug caps and the plug leads with number tags are correct.

Because this Iris Blue car is a 1600 Mark I De Luxe, it has a number of unusual features: a different master cylinder with separate reservoirs for brake and clutch; a dynamo-mounted coil; and Twin Cam style removable access panels in the inner front wings (found on the early Mark I De Luxe only).

This car has been prepared to concours standard – the carburettors would not have been polished originally. The heat shield and the inlet manifold balance pipe are correctly finished in engine colour.

capacity of 1489cc (73.025 × 88.9mm) and the first car in which it was fitted was the MG Magnette ZA, introduced at the 1953 Motor Show. During 1954, the same basic engine was installed also in the new Morris Oxford Series II and the Austin A50 Cambridge. The first MGA engine was originally type BP15GB, but during 1957 the style of engine number prefix was changed to 15GB-U-H, where U indicated a centre gearchange and H stood for high compression. In January 1959, the MGA 1500 was fitted with the revised engine type 15GD-U-H, from car/chassis 61504.

In May 1959 the MGA 1600 followed, with the engine bored out to 75.39mm for a capacity increase to 1588cc. This engine was type 16GA-U-H or 16GA-U, often without a final letter for compression; in any case, the 1489cc and 1588cc MGA engines were only available with one compression ratio, of 8.3:1. On the 1600 Mark II model in April 1961, the bore was further increased to 76.2mm, for a capacity of 1622cc. The resulting engine was type 16GC-U-H (with high compression of 8.9:1) or 16GC-U-L (with low compression of 8.3:1). For brevity, engine number prefixes will often be quoted in abbreviated form, such as 15GB, in this book.

As the pushrod engines were all basically similar, they will be dealt with in one section. Both cylinder head and cylinder block were made of cast iron. The block extended well below the centreline of the crankshaft and was finished off with a simple pressed steel sump. The crankshaft ran in three main bearings of the steel-backed white-metal (later lead-indium) type. The camshaft was mounted low down on the cylinder block on the left-hand side and was driven by chain. The camshaft also ran in three steel-backed white-metal bearings. Tappets, pushrods and rockers operated the valves which were vertical and set in line in the cylinder head. On the 1489cc and 1588cc engines, the diameter of the inlet valve heads was 38.1mm and of the exhaust valve heads 32.54mm. On the 1622cc engine, valve sizes were increased to (approximately) 39.7mm for the inlet valves and 34.17mm for the exhaust valves. All standard pushrod engines had camshafts giving the following valve timing: inlet opens, 16° BTDC; inlet closes, 56° ABDC; exhaust opens, 51° BBDC; exhaust closes, 21° ATDC.

The oil pump, distributor and rev counter were all driven from the camshaft. The solid-skirt aluminium alloy pistons were fitted with three compression rings and an oil control ring. The connecting rod big end bearings were the steel-backed lead-indium or lead-tin type.

The cylinder head had two inlet ports (siamesed for the front and rear pairs of cylinders) and three exhaust ports (serving the front, middle two and rear cylinders). The ports were all on the left-hand side, sharing space with the pushrods. On the left-hand side of the cylinder block were two side covers or tappet covers. Because the contemporary Austin Cambridge still used a mechanical fuel pump, the 15GB engine had a hole on the left-hand side of the cylinder block with a blanking plate where the fuel pump would have been found, but

On the 1600 Mark II De Luxe, the ignition coil was still dynamo-mounted, unlike other pushrod cars of the time. The yellow fan is typical of at least the Mark II models – but may also be original on some 1600 Mark I models. This left-hand drive car has a brake pipe running across the car number plate. Neither the type nor location of the windscreen washer bottle is correct on this car.

The same Mark II De Luxe engine seen from the carburettor side. This car is very original, as one would expect from a low mileage car with known history.

On the left is the original 15GB-type engine, with the blanking plate over the fuel pump hole – redundant in an MGA – removed. On the right is the 15GD-type block, which does not have this hole.

on the 15GD and all 1600 engines the fuel pump boss was left intact and so there was no need for a blanking plate. The 15GB and 15GD engines had the legend '1500' cast on the left-hand side of the crankcase at the front, 16GA engines had '1600' and on 16GC engines this was changed to '1622'. Cylinder heads of both 1489cc and 1588cc engines had the number '15' cast at the rear; only on the 1622cc cylinder heads was this altered to '16'.

All the electrical ancillaries were found on the right-hand side of the engine, including the spark plugs, the distributor, the dynamo and the starter motor. An important difference between the 15GB and 15GD engines was that the position of the starter motor was raised on the latter, necessitating a new gearbox mounting plate as well as a new gearbox tunnel, right-hand toeboard and carpet. Also on the right-hand side of the engine was the dipstick and the external full-flow oil filter – either a Tecalemit or a Purolator type – with its pipework. The water pump, fan and dynamo were driven by belt from the crankshaft front pulley. The engine number was reverse-stamped on a plate rivetted on to a lip at the top of the cylinder block on the right-hand side, just below the plugs between cylinders two and three.

MGA engines were finished in a dark shade of red or maroon, including block, head, sump and rocker cover, as well as thermostat housing, front cover, pulleys, vacuum pipe for advance/retard, carburettor balance pipe,

The 1622 engine (left) is distinguished by having this number cast in. On the right, the 1600 engine (of 1588cc to be precise) has the sump correctly painted red.

heat shield, oil filter housing and water pump, but unfortunately no precise colour reference or mixing formula has been found. The rocker cover had the bayonet-type oil filler cap towards the front. The cap, held by a wire and finished in cadmium plating, was embossed with the brand names of eight recommended lubricants. On early cars another type of cap may be found, with a separate top plate where the oil names were printed black on a tan background. At the rear of the rocker cover were two rectangular plates, on the right-hand side with the MG badge, on the left-hand side listing numbers of those patents which were employed in the design of the engine, including certain Weslake patents. Bolted over the rear of the carburettor balance pipe was a brass plate giving the firing order of 1-3-4-2 and the valve rocker clearance (when hot) of .017in

Five types of pistons which may be encountered on the MGA. At rear left is the late low compression Twin Cam piston, with the original high compression Twin Cam piston at rear right. In the front row, from the left, are a standard 1500 piston, an 8.9:1 high compression 1622cc engine piston, and a 10.1:1 compression piston (available for tuning the 1500 engine).

(1500 models) or .015in (1600 models). The engine mounting brackets were painted black.

The list of change points by engine numbers in the accompanying panel gives details of most of the changes affecting the engine and powertrain in general, excepting certain changes which can not be referred to a specific engine number, or minor changes which typically did not affect parts interchangeability. Because none of the MGA production records quote engine numbers for individual cars, it is usually not possible to cross-reference changes by engine numbers to car/chassis numbers, and some of the dates assigned to changes by engine numbers are approximate.

PRODUCTION CHANGES BY ENGINE NUMBERS

MGA 1500 (15GB type engine)

101 (May 55)
First 15GB engine (start of production, car/chassis 10101).

259 (Oct 55)
Timing chain tensioner added, front engine plate and cover modified to suit.

487 (Nov 55)
Windowless yoke type dynamo introduced.

744 (Dec 55)
Gearbox rear extension oil seal modified to second type with rubber seal and felt washer instead of leather seal and felt washer.

1809 (Feb 56)
Distributor type DM.2.P4 with pre-tilted contact breakers introduced (part no. 1H811), cable run modified.

3289 (Mar 56)
Gearbox mounting plate modified, with oil escape recess and groove machined in front face, to prevent oil leaking on to clutch.

3511 (Apr 56)
Main bearings modified.

4046 (Apr 56)
Increased diameter exhaust valve throats and shorter valve guides.

4525 (May 56)
Clutch withdrawal lever modified with larger diameter pivot bolt.

5504 (May 56)
Pushrod ends increased in diameter, tappets modified to suit.

5682 (Jun 56)
Chromium-plated piston top rings introduced.

6615 (Jun 56)
Diameter of oil return thread to crankshaft rear main bearing reduced.

6625 (Jun 56)
Vacuum pipe to distributor modified to incorporate fuel trap.

7538(?) (Jul 56)
Improved material spec. for water outlet elbow.

7981 (Jul 56)
Gearbox front end cover improved and oil seal fitted, with attendant changes.

8570 (Aug 56)
Connecting rods and caps modified.

10990 (Oct 56)
Gearbox rear extension oil seal modified to third type with leather seal and leather washer.

11298 (Oct 56)
Adaptor for external oil pipe modified.

11301 (Oct 56)
Vacuum pipe for distributor modified.

11935 (Oct 56)
Rear tappet cover modified.

12723 (Nov 56)
Cylinder head heater outlet increased in diameter to reduce restriction in flow.

15688 (Jan 57)
Cylinder head gasket changed from steel/asbestos to copper/asbestos.

16226 (Feb 57)
Stronger clutch pressure plate springs fitted to reduce clutch slip, clutch cover modified to suit.

17061 (Feb 57)
Dynamo pulley reduced in diameter and fan belt shortened to increase dynamo speed.

17151 (Mar 57)
Enlarged inlet port necks in cylinder head.

17538 (?) (Mar 57)
Thermostat modified.

18418 (Mar 57)
Valve rocker cover joint increased in thickness to improve oil sealing.

19383 (Apr 57)
Improved second/third gear synchronizer.

20501 (May 57)
Copper ferrules fitted to cylinder head gasket.

23000 (Jun 57)
Approximate point at which style of engine number prefix changed from BP15GB to 15GB-U-H (approximately at car/chassis 33000).

23448 (Jun 57)
Inlet valve guides modified. Also found on engine numbers 23175 to 23200 inclusive.

25112 (Jul 57)
Gearbox rear extension oil seal, leather type replaced by synthetic rubber type with leather washer (fourth type).

26934 (Aug 57)
New type of Tecalemit oil filter, Purolator oil filter introduced as alternative, and oil filter seal modified. This change also applied to engine numbers from 26661 to 26700 inclusive.

27909 (Sep 57)
Pistons and rings modified.

28979 (Sep 57)
Oil dipstick minimum mark raised from $^3/_4$ in to $^3/_8$ in below the maximum mark.

29710 (Oct 57)
Modified bracket for ignition coil mounting on dynamo.

35809 (Jan 58)
Front tappet cover and crankshaft vent pipe modified.

38484 (Feb 58)
Heavier gudgeon pins with smaller centre holes, pistons modified.

39526 (Mar 58)
Water pump with one-piece bearing introduced. This was also found on engine numbers 39365 to 39400 inclusive.

40105 (Mar 58)
Two holes drilled in oil cavity in cylinder block rear main bearing cap and cutaway machined in oil return housing. Drainpipe discontinued.

40825 (Apr 58)
Pistons with deeper grooves and rings of increased radial thickness to decrease oil consumption.

45412 (Aug 58)
Gearbox rear extension oil seal, leather washer replaced by felt washer (fifth type).

45905 (Aug 58)
Modified bracket for ignition coil mounting on dynamo.

46342 (Sep 58)
Oil pump suction pipe moved forward to prevent starvation when cornering or braking. Pump, strainer and studs all modified. This change also applied to engine numbers from 46045 to 46100 inclusive.

47901 (Oct 58)
Tappet adjusting screw locknuts modified.

48911 (Nov 58)
Rocker shaft brackets modified.

51767 (Jan 59)
Final engine number in 15GB series.

MGA 1500 (15GD type engine)

101 (Jan 59)
15GD type engine introduced at car/chassis 61504. No blanking plate for mechanical fuel pump; new high starter position. Gearbox modified (mounting plate, casing and rear extension). Propeller shaft with splined sliding joint at front.

6530 (Apr 59)
Connecting rod bearings modified.

7816 (May 59)
Final engine number in 15GD series.

MGA 1600 (16GA type engine)

101 (May 59)
16GA type introduced at start of 1600 model, car/chassis 68851. Gearbox modified to prevent disengagement of third gear.

4788 (Aug 59)
Thermostat modified.

6272 (Sep 59)
New dynamo type C.40/1 introduced, control box modified with introduction of Lucar connectors to dynamo harness (coinciding with car/chassis 74489). New fan belt. New ignition coil bracket.

6396 (Sep 59)
Dynamo pulley and fan belt modified.

9649 (Oct 59)
Dipstick cranked away from crankcase for better accessibility.

12834 (Dec 59)
Gearbox front cover bosses modified (cp Twin-Cam engine number 2228).

20846 (Apr 60)
Exhaust valves of improved material.

21705 (Apr 60)
Connecting rods with thicker webs, bearing caps modified.

21805 (Apr 60)
Crankshaft modified to increase oil return scroll clearance to cylinder block. Introduction of VP3 lead-indium main bearings in place of white metal type.

25740 (Jun 60)
Thicker, stiffer cylinder block side covers to reduce the possibility of oil leaks.

31640 (Mar 61)
Exhaust valve outer springs modified.

31660 (Mar 61)
Final engine number in 16GA series.

MGA 1600 Mark II (16GC type engine)

101 (Mar 61)
16GC engine introduced at start of 1600 Mark II model, car/chassis 100352. New distributor type DM.2 with rolling weight centrifugal advance mechanism. Gearbox casing modified, welch plugs deleted.

127 (Mar 61)
Low compression engine pistons modified.

1012 (May 61)
Low compression engine distributor modified.

2327 (Jul 61)
Oil gallery plugs commonalised. Also on engine numbers 2157 to 2225 inclusive.

3708 (Sep 61)
Lighter flywheel introduced.

3929 (Oct 61)
Gearbox first motion shaft with involute splines formed by rolling, giving stronger spline section at reduced cost; clutch driven plate modified to suit (this change coincides with car/chassis 104022 for cars with high compression engines, and 104468 for those with low compression engines).

4004 (Oct 61)
High compression engine distributor modified.

4748 (Nov 61)
Gearbox casing of thicker section around bellhousing and incorporating stiffening ribs to reduce vibration. Longer bolts between bellhousing and engine.

5403 (Dec 61)
Reverse gear assembly modified.

6435 (Jan 62)
Starter motor modified.

8263 (Apr 62)
Crankshaft front oil thrower and crankshaft front pulley modified. Engine front cover felt oil seal replaced by rubber oil seal.

8422 (Apr 62)
High compression engine distributor and cover modified.

8851 (May 62)
Final engine number in 16GC series.

The header tank is black on this car but can also be found unpainted on a Twin Cam. There is only just enough room for the heater air intake hose, and the ignition coil is hidden behind it.

TWIN CAM ENGINE

Initial designs for the Twin Cam engine were undertaken in 1955 when two different engine proposals, one developed by Austin and the other by Morris Engines at Coventry, were fitted to two of the Tourist Trophy race cars. Only the car with the Morris-designed engine started, but it did not finish the race. The production version which appeared in 1958 was developed from the Morris Engines design and was loosely based on the pushrod B-series, although it was very different at the end of the day.

Dimensions of 75.39 × 88.9mm were shared with the MGA 1600 pushrod engine which appeared during the following year. The block was of cast iron but the cylinder head was of aluminium alloy. The crankshaft had three main bearings (lead-tin or lead-indium type) and drove a half-speed layshaft on the left-hand side of the engine through a pair of reduction gears. This half-speed shaft occupied the location where you would expect to find the camshaft on a pushrod MGA engine. The oil pump, distributor and rev counter were driven from the half-speed shaft.

The half-speed shaft drove the two camshafts in the cylinder head through 3/8in pitch duplex roller chain, which ran over a fixed idler sprocket and was fitted with an adjustable tensioner. Each camshaft ran in three white-metal bearings, the inlet camshaft on the right and the exhaust camshaft on the left. The camshafts activated the valves through inverted bucket type tappets with shim adjustment. The valves were set at an included angle of 80°. Valve diameters were 40.38mm for inlet and 36.58mm for exhaust valves. The valve timing was as follows: inlet opens, 20° BTDC; inlet closes, 50° ABDC; exhaust opens, 50° BBDC; exhaust closes, 20° ATDC. One contemporary source (the American *Car and Driver* magazine for June 1959) claimed that the first 40 Twin Cam engines had wider overlap camshafts with valve timing of 35°/65°/65°/35°, but it has not been possible to establish this with certainty. The solid-skirt aluminium pistons had conical tops (with lower domed tops on the later low compression pistons) and were fitted with three compression rings, an oil control ring and on later engines also with an expander ring.

There were siamesed inlet ports on the right-hand side of the cylinder head, and four separate exhaust ports on the left-hand side, with two exhaust manifolds. The distributor was fitted on the left-hand side of the front engine cover and the plugs were in the centre of the cylinder head. The high-

The well-filled Twin Cam engine bay shows the most frequently encountered plug lead route at the front of the engine. This car is an early Twin Cam with 1500-style body, and thus has the extra flasher relay behind the heater. The heater is the other way round compared to the pushrod cars. The sealing strip on top of the radiator is unique to the Twin Cam. This car has the early washer bottle with narrow neck, and the blue colour for the bottle bracket is correct.

The carburettor air filters disappear virtually out of sight. These pictures will give a generally good idea of how inferior the Twin Cam is to the pushrod cars when it comes to under-bonnet accessibility.

tension ignition cables were re-routed from the side to the front of the engine from engine number 556. The dipstick was held in a bracket on the rear left-hand corner of the engine and went through an external tube into the cast-alloy sump.

The dynamo, starter motor and oil filter were all on the right-hand side of the engine. The engine number was prefixed by the type designation 16GB-U and was found on a plate rivetted to the rear end of the cylinder block, just in front of the bellhousing.

The Twin Cam cylinder block and head were finished in red, including the sump, the engine front cover, the inlet manifolds and the heat shield, while the camshaft covers were finished in natural aluminium. An MG badge was cast in each cam cover at the front, with the letters and the octagon picked out in red. The screw-in oil filler cap was on the left-hand cam cover adjacent to the MG logo.

The Twin Cam engine acquired a reputation for unreliability in service. With the high compression ratio of 9.9:1 it was rather sensitive to fuel, and if low-octane fuel was used or if the ignition was advanced too far, piston burning was likely to occur. The engine was extremely willing to rev, even beyond the safe limit, which could easily lead to close encounters between valves and piston crowns. A third problem concerned oil consumption: this was high, particularly on early engines, and owners did not always check the oil level frequently enough, perhaps because the dipstick was not easily accessible and was awkward to use.

Most of the changes to the Twin Cam engine – detailed in the accompanying list of change points by engine numbers – concerned attempts to reduce oil consumption, by means of frequent changes to pistons and rings. Towards the end of production, more drastic action was taken on two fronts. A distributor without vacuum advance was fitted from engine number 2223, and dealers were advised to fit all earlier cars with this type to avoid over-advancing and consequent piston failure. Then at engine number 2251, lower-domed pistons with a compression ratio of 8.3:1 were introduced, and these were subsequently used for all rebuilt engines. Power was reduced slightly, from 108bhp to 100bhp, but reliability was undoubtedly improved. At the same time stronger valve springs were fitted.

In later years, many Twin Cams were fitted with the low compression pistons and other modifications. A properly-rebuilt Twin Cam engine used sensibly should be perfectly reliable, but quite a few Twin Cams have had their original engines replaced with pushrod MGA engines in cases where owners had to give up for lack of spare parts. Fitting a pushrod engine in a Twin Cam is fairly straightforward, but it is rather more difficult to fit the physically larger Twin Cam engine in a pushrod car – even though this has been known to occur in a few instances.

Production Changes by Engine Numbers

Twin Cam

101 (Apr 58)
First engine (start of production, car/chassis 501).

131 (Jun 58)
Radiator overflow pipe modified.

141 (Jun 58)
Possible change of camshafts and valve timing (see text).

194 (Jun 58)
Thermostat with lower opening temperature.

272 (Sep 58)
Smaller dynamo pulley and shorter fan belt to alter dynamo speed and increase charging rate.

313 (Oct 58)
Layshaft oil pump gear and oil pump spindle with more teeth.

446 (Nov 58)
Pistons with twin-segment scraper ring to reduce oil consumption.

448 (Nov 58)
Dynamo adjusting link changed.

556 (Dec 58)
Ignition cables lengthened and re-routed round front of cylinder head.

574 (Dec 58)
Water inlet pipe straightened.

581 (Dec 58)
Water inlet elbow lengthened.

606 (Dec 58)
Modified top ring to pistons to overcome piston noise.

657 (Dec 58)
Cylinder block rear side cover breather pipe modified to prevent oil leaking on to exhaust system.

1087 (Feb 59)
Tappets increased in length by 0.25in to 1.5in to eliminate risk of fractures.

1343 (Mar 59)
Connecting rods modified with bosses at small end for balancing purposes. Heavier big end bearing caps.

1379 (Mar 59)
Close-ratio gearbox introduced as an option. When fitted with this gearbox, engine prefix should be 16GB-Da.

? (Apr 59)
N.3 spark plugs introduced to reduce heat at piston crown.

1587 (Apr 59)
Cast-iron sleeves introduced for tappet bores in cylinder head to reduce wear.

? (Jul 59)
Shorter carburettor damper pistons for improved even running and maximum speed. These are identified by the carburettor caps being stamped 'O'.

2057 (Jul 59)
Pistons with modified scraper ring and expander ring added. These were also fitted to a few earlier engines.

2211 (Dec 59)
Tappets modified.

2223 (Jan 60)
New type distributor less vacuum unit, to prevent over-advancing with possible consequent piston failure. Supposedly retro-fitted by campaign change to all earlier cars. Coincides with car/chassis 2561.

2228 (Jan 60)
Gearbox front cover bosses modified (cp. 16GA engine number 12834).

2251 (Mar 60)
Alternative low compression pistons (8.3:1) introduced, with resulting decrease in power from 108bhp to 100bhp. High and low compression pistons fitted with plain instead of chromium-plated top rings. Stronger valve springs fitted. Coincides with car/chassis 2609.

? (Mar 60)
Crankshaft main bearings and big end bearings of lead-tin type introduced as alternatives.

2272 (May 60)
Estimated final Twin Cam engine number

Please note that because of limited production it is very difficult to cross-reference Twin Cam engine numbers to car/chassis numbers and thus build dates.

Exchange Engines

It is worth including a few notes on exchange engines. BMC originally supplied completely re-conditioned replacement engines (in later years known as the 'Gold Seal' engines) for all MGA models, with very distinctive engine number prefixes. These prefixes were in fact the part numbers of the stripped engine units as quoted in the Service Parts Lists. The following are these part numbers for the exchange engines.

MGA 1500, 15GB engines: without timing chain tensioner (engine numbers 101 to 258), 8G207; with timing chain tensioner (engine numbers 259 to 51767), originally 8G210, later 'rationalized' units 48G362R. MGA 1500, 15GD engines with high starter position (engine numbers 101 to 7816), originally 48G165R, later 'rationalized' units 48G361R, in parts lists also quoted as 48G301R (presumably one of the above numbers is a printing error in original BMC literature!). MGA 1600 and 1600 Mark II: 16GA engines 1588cc (engine numbers 101 to 31660) 48G157R; 16GC engines 1622cc (engine numbers 101 to 8851), 8.9:1 compression 48G214R, 8.3:1 compression 48G218R. MGA Twin Cam, 16GB type engines: AEH 37.

Quite a few MGA cars have over the years acquired B-series engines from a variety of other sources. Most other B-series engines are a fairly simple fit in an MGA, except those from the MG Magnette ZA/ZB, Wolseley 15/50 and certain light commercial vehicles which have very different sumps and oil pump pick-up points. The only saloon car engines which originally had a mechanical rev counter drive were those fitted to Riley models (1.5, 4/68 and 4/72 to 1966), types 15R and 16R. Some MGAs in North America ended up with Metropolitan 1500 engines – types 1H, 15F or 15N – while in the UK the most common alternative engines are from the Austin/Morris/Wolseley 1622cc Farina saloons, types 16AMW or 16AA, between 1961-71. Another common swap is an MGB engine, usually the three-bearing types with prefixes starting 18G or 18GA. An MGA owner or prospective purchaser who is in doubt should try to verify the engine number as seen on the engine, and beware engine number plates which look as if they have been tampered with, or which are brand new.

Exhaust System

All pushrod cars had a single three-branch manifold and a single downpipe, leading to a pipe running back on the left-hand side of the car with a simple tubular silencer towards the rear, and two mounting brackets in front of and at the rear of the silencer respectively. The only variation concerned late 1600 Mark II cars exported to Switzerland from car/chassis 108405: these had an additional silencer introduced in the front pipe to comply with local legislation.

The Twin Cam exhaust system was also on the left-hand side of the car. It had two exhaust manifolds and downpipes. The front downpipe served the front and rear cylinders and the rear downpipe served the two middle cylinders. The dual front exhaust pipe merged into one, well in front of the silencer. The silencer was similar to that found on pushrod cars but was of a slightly different type as the pipe diameter was bigger.

The two different types of ignition coil mounting. On the left, the bracket which attached to the right-hand engine mounting found on the 1600 and Mark II models (except De Luxe versions). On the right, the dynamo fixing bracket found on the 1500 models and De Luxe versions of later cars.

Exhaust manifolds were left unpainted on all cars, with pipes and silencers painted aluminium. There were no changes to the exhaust system during the production run of either the pushrod cars or of the Twin Cam.

IGNITION SYSTEM

A normal coil and distributor system was used on all models. The 1500 at first had a distributor type DM2, but from engine number 15GB/1809 the modified unit type DM2.P4 with pre-tilted contact breakers was introduced. This was carried over on the 1600 model, and was also originally used on the Twin Cam. While the 1600 Mark II distributor was basically of the same type, the original toggle-type centrifugal advance mechanism was replaced on this model by a rolling weight mechanism. On the 1500 model, a fuel trap was incorporated in the distributor vacuum pipe from engine number 15GB/6625.

On later Twin Cam cars, from engine number 2223, the DM2.P4 distributor was replaced by a type 23D4 which was not fitted with a vacuum advance unit. This modification was introduced to overcome the problem of Twin Cam ignition timing being over-advanced with possible piston failure as a result. It was recommended that the later type distributor was fitted to all earlier Twin Cam cars.

The ignition coil was a type HA12 on all MGA cars and only the location differed. On the 1500, it was mounted with a clamp bracket to the dynamo, but on 1600 and 1600 Mark II cars it was mounted with a bracket on the right-hand front engine mounting. The exceptions were the 1600 and 1600 Mark II De Luxe models, on which the coil was again mounted on the dynamo. On the Twin Cam the coil was mounted on the left-hand inner wing panel behind the heater air intake hose.

Originally, Champion NA.8 plugs were recommended for the 1500 but this type of plug was later re-numbered N.5, which was quoted for all subsequent models. On the Twin Cam, N.5 plugs were quoted at first for standard road work, with N.3 plugs being recommended for high-speed running. Later on, the N.3 type was recommended for all types of usage. For competition use, N.58R plugs were recommended on the Twin Cam. On all cars, Lucas suppressors number 78106A were fitted integral with the push-on plug caps.

The plug gap for all pushrod engined cars was .024-.026in (.625-.660mm), while on the Twin Cam it was .025in (.64mm). The points gap was .014-.016in (.35-.40mm) for all cars. Static ignition timing was 7° BTDC on 1500 and 1600 models. On the 1600 Mark II model it was 10° BTDC on all low compression engines and on high compression engines up to engine number 16GC-U-H/4003. Later 16GC-U-H engines had ignition timing of 5° BTDC. On the Twin Cam with the high compression engine (9.9:1) static ignition timing was TDC, while for the low compression engine (8.3:1) it was 8° BTDC. The firing order was 1-3-4-2 on all cars.

COOLING SYSTEM

All cars had a normal pressurised thermo-siphon system assisted by pump and fan, and regulated by a thermostat. The original 1500 water pump was replaced from engine number 15GB/39526 by a new pump with a one-piece bearing, this pump being carried forward to the 1600 model and fitted to pushrod cars to the end of production. The same six-bladed fan was found on all cars, including the Twin Cam. It was painted black on early 1500 models, but was changed to red in 1958. Most Twin Cam and 1600 models had red fans. On the 1600 Mark II, and possibly some late 1600 models, the fans were yellow. BMC replacement fans were typically black.

The Smiths thermostat (type X.85025) was set to open at 74°C, but an alternative thermostat supplied for countries with cold climates had an opening temperature of 86°C. On cars supplied to hot climates the thermostat might be omitted altogether and replaced by a blanking sleeve. The thermostat was modified at 1500 engine number 15GB/17538 (or possibly at 7538 when the water elbow outlet was changed), but the new thermostat was interchangeable with the old. The thermostat was changed again at 1600 engine number 16GA/4788, but the modified type was still interchangeable.

A common radiator with integral header tank, painted flat black, was found on all pushrod-engined cars and was not changed during the entire production run. However, from 1600 car/chassis 71832 the filler cap was

At the rear, the Twin Cam carburettors with larger throat diameters and longer inlet tracts, with the special Twin Cam air filter adjacent. The pushrod air filter and carburettors are in front.

Another difference between Twin Cam and pushrod cars. The larger fuel pump (left) is the Twin Cam type with the large box-shaped body. The rubber cover at front left was fitted until May 1960.

upgraded from 4lbs to 7lbs pressure, and the filler cap was changed again at car/chassis 88192, with the later type being recommended also for earlier cars. All filler caps were of the eared bayonet-fitting type. The feed pipe to the heater on cars so fitted ran back along the left-hand side of the rocker cover and was finished in natural copper.

On the Twin Cam, the radiator had to be mounted slightly further forward as the Twin Cam engine was longer. In consequence, there was no room for an integral header tank on this model, so the Twin Cam radiator was totally different. The Twin Cam had a remote header tank, an aluminium casting sometimes painted black, found on the left-hand side of the engine above the exhaust manifolds. The overflow pipe was modified at Twin Cam engine number 131, and from car/chassis 652 a totally different overflow pipe was fitted, incorporating a 7lbs relief valve. At the same time the filler cap was changed from the MGA 1500 type rated at 4lbs to a simple non-pressurised fixed cap. The relief valve was fitted to prevent loss of coolant due to engine vibration transmitted to the valve in the filler cap. The Twin Cam water pump was entirely different from the standard type. Originally the Twin Cam had the same thermostat as the standard car (part number 11G291) with an opening temperature of 74°C, but from engine number 194 a thermostat opening at 50-55°C was fitted, and was recommended for replacement purposes also on earlier cars. A rubber strip air seal was fitted to the top of the Twin Cam radiator.

Carburettors & Fuel System

The rear-mounted fuel tank was the same on all MGA models, and held 10 gallons (12 US gallons or 45.4 litres). It was painted black and was attached to the chassis by two strap and mounting assemblies, also black, which were bolted to the crossmember above the rear axle, and to the tubular crossmember at the rear of the chassis. The fuel pipe and the fuel gauge sender unit were both on the right-hand side of the tank. The filler neck was in the right-hand rear top corner of the tank, with a hose connection to the filler extension through the boot, emerging on the rear tonneau panel by the lower right-hand corner of the boot lid. The stainless steel filler cap was spring-loaded, being released by a small tab marked 'lift' mounted opposite the hinge.

Listed as part of the competition equip-

The pedal arrangement on a left-hand drive 1500 model. The original carpet correctly has edge binding only around the chassis cross-member, and the heel mat is the correct type.

On this right-hand drive 1600, modern carpet has been fitted with extra edge binding and a reproduction heel mat. Note the rubber cover bulge behind the clutch pedal to clear the starter motor Bendix drive, and the dipswitch positioned above this. Originally the dipswitch was lower down.

ment were alternative fuel tanks of 15 or 17 gallons capacity, and a quick-release filler cap of the so-called 'Le Mans' type. There was also a 20 gallon tank which was regularly fitted to the works competition cars. It should be noted that to obtain correct readings on the fuel gauge, it was necessary to fit special sender units and fuel gauges if any of these larger tanks were fitted.

The fuel pump was mounted on a bracket on the tubular chassis crossmember on the right-hand side directly behind the heelboard, and was accessible from the tonneau area when the hood stowage compartment floor (the battery cover panel) was removed. The fuel pump was an electric SU high pressure pump (HP-type). On pushrod cars the specification of the pump was originally AUA 54, but from car/chassis 100612, early in the 1600 Mark II production run, it was upgraded to specification AUA 154, with an improved diaphragm assembly and other smaller changes. A rubber cover was originally fitted to the fuel pump but this was discontinued at car/chassis 93225.

The Twin Cam had a rather different fuel pump, a large capacity type LCS to specification AUA 73. This pump had a box-shaped as opposed to cylindrical body. The Twin Cam fuel pump delivery rate was 12.5 gallons per hour, rather better than the pushrod cars with a delivery rate of 10 gallons per hour. All Twin Cam models had the rubber cover over the pump, and there was no change to the fuel pump on this model. The De Luxe models had the standard pushrod car type fuel pump, not the Twin Cam pump.

The fuel pipe ran forward along the right-hand chassis side member held by inverted 'U' clips inside the floorboard rail, and as the pushrod cars had their carburettors on the left-hand side the fuel pipe had to cross over on the horizontal shelf behind the engine. All fuel pipes were plated carbon steel. On the Twin Cam, the pipe fed directly to the rear carburettor on the right-hand side of the car. The flexible pipes from the main feed pipe to the rear carburettor, and between the carburettors, were braided steel Petroflex from Smiths.

All pushrod-engined cars had two SU H.4 semi-downdraught carburettors, of $1^1/_2$ in diameter and fitted with .090in jets. The standard needle for the 1500 was type GS, (richer CC, weaker number 4), while on 1600 and 1600 Mark II models a standard needle number 6 was used. There were some slight changes to the carburettors during the 1600 production run, but there is no record of when they occurred, and it appears that the old and new parts were interchangeable. All carburettors – including those on the Twin Cam – had hexagonal brass tops. The carburettor balance pipe was painted engine colour. There were individual air cleaners for each carburettor, of the round pancake Vokes type, with an oil-wetted element. The air cleaners were finished in black.

The Twin Cam had HD.6 carburettors of $1^3/_4$ in diameter, with .100in jets. The standard needle was OA6, with RH for rich running or OA7 for weak running. From July 1959, the Twin Cam was fitted with shorter damper pistons (reduced in length from .378in to .308in) for improved even running and maximum speed. The part number was changed from AUC8103 to AUC8114. No change point is recorded, but these later damper pistons can be identified by the carburettor tops being stamped 'O'. Twin Cams had a different type of Vokes air cleaner, of an elongated oval shape. The air cleaners were modified from Twin Cam car/chassis 2468 by a venturi being incorporated in each air cleaner. Otherwise the Twin Cam fuel system was not subjected to any change.

Engine controls were similar on all models, allowing for variations between right-hand drive and left-hand drive cars, and for the Twin Cam having its carburettors on the opposite side. All cars had a pendant accelerator pedal with a small square pad with vertical grooves. On the 1500 model from car/chassis 24594, an auxiliary return spring was added to the throttle cable. On left-hand drive cars the accelerator pedal was mounted on a cross-shaft assembly which was of a slightly different type on the Twin Cam, and the Twin Cam type of cross-shaft was found also on the De Luxe models.

For details of the larger carburettors available for tuning pushrod engined cars, please refer to the separate sections found later in this book dealing with special tuning and competition equipment.

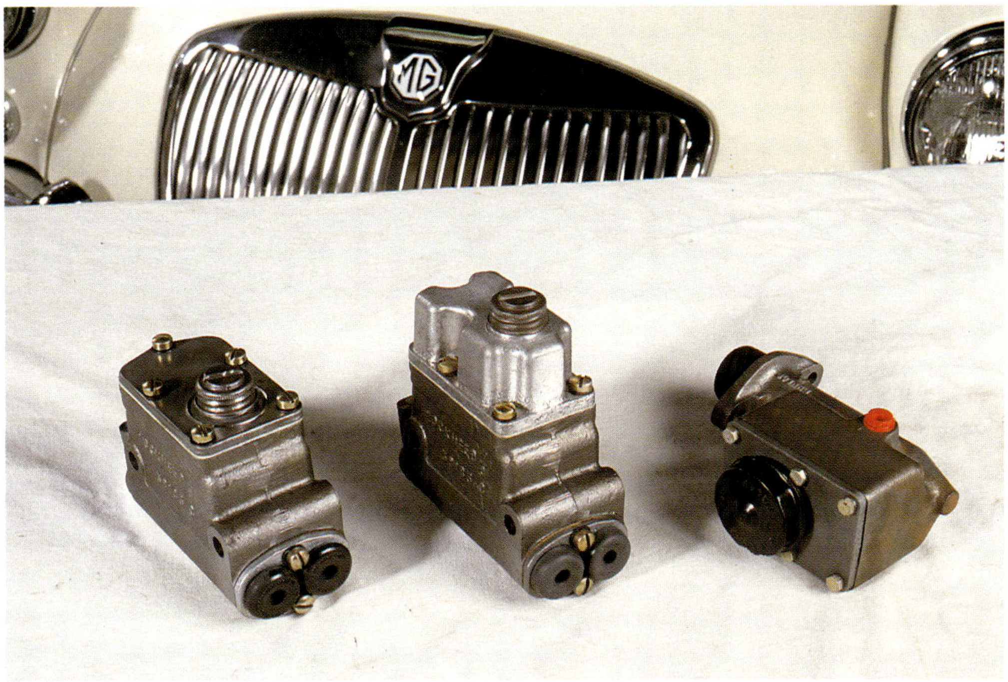

The three main types of master cylinder found on MGA cars, from left: 1500 type; 1600 and Mark II type with a raised cover; and Twin Cam or De Luxe type, turned on its side.

CLUTCH

All MGA cars used an 8in Borg & Beck single dry-plate clutch with hydraulic operation, type A6-G on pushrod-engined cars, type 8ARG on the Twin Cam. Pushrod-engined cars – except the De Luxe models – used a common hydraulic fluid reservoir and combined master cylinder for brakes and clutch, while on Twin Cam and De Luxe models there was a separate master cylinder for the clutch.

On the MGA 1500, stronger pressure springs and a modified cover assembly were fitted from engine number 15GB/16226, while on the 1600 Mark II the clutch driven plate was modified from engine number 16GC/3929 to suit a modified gearbox first motion shaft with finer splines (see gearbox section). The clutch withdrawal lever was modified at engine number 15GB/4525, with a larger diameter clutch fork pivot bolt. Factory Service Memorandum MG/226 issued in July 1958 stated that an alternative design of clutch driven plate with four instead of six damper springs had been introduced 'recently', but failed to record the change point. The 1500 Parts List does not give an alternative part number for the driven plate assembly, and always shows the type of plate with six springs anyway. Otherwise the clutch was not subject to any important changes during the production run.

The clutch pedal was of the pendant type, with a shield-shaped rubber pad carrying vertical ribs, matching the brake pedal. The clutch pedal was modified on left-hand drive MGA 1500s from car/chassis 58713, on right-hand drive cars from 61100. The pedal itself was different on Twin Cam and De Luxe models, but the pedal rubber was the same.

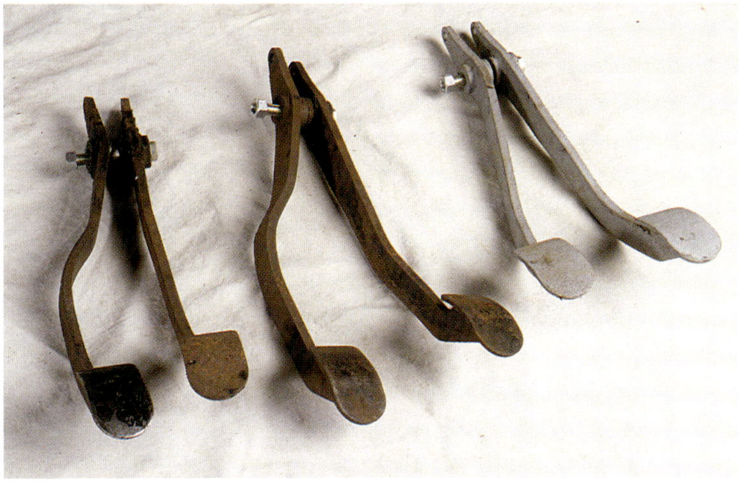

Three patterns of clutch and brake pedals, from an early right-hand drive 1500 (left), a later right-hand drive 1500 or 1600 model (centre) and a left-hand drive car (right). On a Twin Cam (or De Luxe), the clutch pedal arm would extend further above the pivot point.

The slave cylinder, situated below the clutch on the right-hand side, was modified on the MGA 1500 from car/chassis 11768 when a simplified housing without a separate banjo was introduced. On the Twin Cam and De Luxe models the slave cylinder was of a completely different design but was not subject to any changes during the production run of these models. Neither was the master cylinder on these cars subject to any important changes.

The combined clutch/brake master cylinder of the standard pushrod-engined cars is dealt with in the braking section.

Gearboxes are very similar; but there are detail points of difference. From left, these are an early 1500 gearbox for a 15GB-type engine with the low starter position, a later 1500 or 1600 gearbox with the high starter position introduced in January 1959 for the 15GD-type engine, a Twin Cam gearbox which has an unused boss for a hydraulic slave cylinder on top of the bellhousing, and a 1600 Mark II gearbox with strengthening ribs on the bellhousing. The Twin Cam gearbox in this picture has the cover plate for the selectors (on the rear extension) mounted the wrong way round.

GEARBOX

The gearbox was the standardized BMC B-series four-speed unit with synchromesh on second, third and fourth gears. The one-piece bellhousing and gearbox casing had a detachable side cover on the left-hand side. The bellhousing and casing were different on the Twin Cam model, with a boss on the bellhousing. There was a separate gearbox extension which also held the rear power unit mount, and on to this was bolted the remote control unit which held the short vertical gearlever. A gearbox dipstick was accommodated on the right-hand side of the gearbox, accessible from inside the car through a rubber plug in the gearbox tunnel, covered by a carpet flap.

The gearbox number was stamped adjacent to the dipstick. Apart from stating that gearboxes were individually numbered, it is unfortunately not possible to be more specific because the gearbox numbers were never listed in the production records for individual cars. It seems that gearboxes had four-figure numbers with varying letter prefixes, but it has not been possible to work out the system, if there was one.

Unfortunately, many of the smaller changes to the gearbox are recorded only by gearbox numbers, especially during the run of the MGA 1500. The reader who needs this detailed information should consult the Service Parts Lists. The gearbox was changed at the start of the 15GD engine series (car/chassis 61504), with changes applying to the casing, the rear extension, the third motion shaft and the layshaft, apart from other less important parts. The later type of 1500 gearbox was carried over on the early 1600 models with few changes, but with the start of the 1600 Mark II model (car/chassis 100352, and the start of the 16GC engine series) the casing assembly was modified. At engine number 16GC/3929, the first motion shaft was given involute splines formed by rolling, and the clutch driven plate was modified to suit. At engine number 16GC/4748 the casing was improved with a thicker section round the bellhousing, and stiffening ribs to reduce vibration.

Although there were detail differences to the Twin Cam gearbox, the internals were for all practical purposes identical to those of the pushrod-engined cars.

One area where there was a slight problem was the oil seal of the gearbox rear extension, with no fewer than five different types being employed in turn on the MGA 1500. The change points for these and other gearbox modifications are detailed in the list of change points by engine numbers, found in

The gearbox tunnel on the left is from an early 1500 model with the 15GB engine. The tunnel on the right has the extra rubber cover 'blip' necessitated by the high starter position introduced with the 15GD engine in January 1959, and found on all later pushrod models as well as on the Twin Cam.

STANDARD GEARBOX

	Gearbox ratios, all models	Overall ratios, 1500/1600/ Twin Cam	Overall ratios, 1600 Mark II
First	3.64:1	15.652:1	14.924:1
Second	2.214:1	9.520:1	9.077:1
Third	1.374:1	5.908:1	5.633:1
Fourth	1.0:1	4.3:1	4.1:1
Reverse	4.76:1	20.468:1	19.516:1

OPTIONAL CLOSE-RATIO GEARBOX

	Gearbox ratios, all models	Overall ratios, 1500/1600/ Twin Cam	Overall ratios, 1600 Mark II
First	2.445:1	10.514:1	10.025:1
Second	1.62:1	6.966:1	6.642:1
Third	1.268:1	5.452:1	5.199:1
Fourth	1.0:1	4.3:1	4.1:1
Reverse	3.199:1	13.756:1	13.116:1

OPTIONAL 4.555:1 REAR AXLE RATIO

	Overall ratios, standard gearbox	Overall ratios, close-ratio gearbox
First	16.580:1	11.137:1
Second	10.085:1	7.379:1
Third	6.259:1	5.776:1
Fourth	4.555:1	4.555:1
Reverse	21.682:1	14.571:1

the section dealing with the pushrod engines earlier in this book.

The standard gear ratios, which were not changed during the MGA production run, are shown in the adjacent panel (the overall ratios quoted for the Mark II model would obviously also apply to any of the earlier cars if fitted with the 4.1:1 rear axle ratio).

A close-ratio gearbox became available as an option at least from April 1959 onwards on the Twin Cam model, and also on pushrod-engined cars from then on. The ratios for this gearbox are shown in the second panel.

On cars which were originally fitted with the close-ratio gearbox, the code letter 'U' (for centre-change gearbox) in the engine number prefix was replaced by the code letters 'Da' (for close-ratio, centre-change gearbox). Originally, the close-ratio gears were fitted into gearbox casings at Abingdon, but from July 1961 they were fitted in gearboxes at Morris Engines Branch in Coventry, undoubtedly due to increased demand for such gearboxes to be fitted in the De Luxe versions of the 1600 Mark II. The close-ratio gearbox was always most commonly found on the Twin Cam and De Luxe models. Close-ratio gear clusters could be supplied for conversion of standard gearboxes (refer to the section on competition equipment).

The 1600 and 1600 Mark II models could be supplied from the factory with the alternative rear axle ratio of 4.555:1 (9/41). Although not quoted in the Parts Lists, this could also be supplied on 1500 and Twin

The only caveat concerning this excellent rear axle view is that the battery cradles are possibly reproduction items, with rounded corners differing slightly from the original. Otherwise this is a fine illustration of the detail and finish of the rear axle and suspension of a typical MGA with rear drum brakes.

Cam models. The third panel shows how the overall gear ratios would change.

Other rear axle ratios could be supplied for competition purposes (see section on competition equipment), and would obviously change the overall gear ratios. None of these alternative ratios was fitted as a production line item. The calculation of overall gear ratios for these other rear axle ratios is left as an exercise for the reader!

On all models the complete gearbox casing – including the bellhousing, rear extension and remote control unit – was left unpainted. The gearlever was chrome-plated and carried a black pear-shaped Bakelite knob, with the shift pattern – the normal H with reverse to the left and back – engraved in white. There was a rubber gaiter around the gearlever where it passed through the carpet.

Propeller Shaft

A short one-piece propeller shaft, painted black, connected gearbox and rear axle. It was made by Hardy Spicer and incorporated universal joints with needle roller bearings front and rear. A reverse-spline sliding joint was fitted between the gearbox output shaft and the front universal joint. On the 1500 model from car/chassis 20753, the propeller shaft was modified and a dust cover was added at the front. A further modification occurred at car/chassis 61504 (and on a few earlier cars), co-inciding with the introduction of engine type 15GD, with a new propeller shaft incorporating a splined sliding joint within the shaft itself, just behind the front universal joint. This propeller shaft was connected to the gearbox with a four-bolt flanged connection, with a similar matching flange on the gearbox output shaft. The new type propeller shaft appears also to have been fitted without any further change to all Twin Cam models from the start of production, as well as to all 1600 and 1600 Mark II models.

Rear Axle

All MGA cars used the basic standardized BMC B-series rear axle, of the three-quarter floating type with hypoid bevel final drive, and a one-piece banjo-type axle casing with a bolt-on nosepiece and differential carrier. The standard rear axle ratio on the 1500, 1600 and Twin Cam models was 4.3:1 (10/43), while on the 1600 Mark II the ratio was raised to 4.1:1 (10/41). The 4.1:1 ratio could also be supplied for earlier models as part of the competition equipment. Quoted as optional equipment on 1600 and 1600 Mark II models – and also available on earlier cars – was a ratio of 4.555:1 (9/41). For competition a ratio of 3.909:1 (11/43) was available, and for the Twin Cam alternative ratios of 4.875:1 (8/39) and 5.125:1 (8/41) were also quoted. The first MGA sales brochure of 1955 mentions a ratio of 3.727:1 (11/41). For calculations of overall ratios with standard rear axle ratios, please refer to the gearbox section.

Disc wheeled and wire wheeled cars had different half shafts and hubs, and the rear axle casing assemblies were slightly modified to suit.

On the 1500 car/chassis 10917 (disc wheeled cars) and 11450 (wire wheeled cars), handed rear hub lock nuts were introduced, with a left-hand thread on the left-hand side of the car. Prior to this, right-hand thread lock nuts had been found on both sides of the car. An additional rubber ring oil seal was fitted to the rear hubs of later 1500 models, with a change point quoted in the Workshop Manual only by axle number.

From the start of 1600 production, the half shafts, hubs and differential wheels were modified when involute splines were adopted for the half shafts. From car/chassis 82893 (disc wheeled cars) and 82749 (wire wheeled cars), changes were made again, when the half shafts were given finer splines at the inboard end (changed from 10 to 25 splines).

The Twin Cam rear axle was modified to suit the rear disc brakes and the special wheels of this model. At car/chassis 1840 the rear hub extensions were modified, and at car/chassis 2371 the half shafts were given involute splines similar to the modification introduced from the start of the 1600 model. The De Luxe versions of the 1600 and 1600 Mark II models carried over the Twin Cam rear axle, subsequently incorporating the modifications introduced on the later 1600 models as detailed above.

All MGA rear axles had a filler plug in the

The correct type of wood rim light-alloy steering wheel (optional on all models) and the standard steering wheel for all models. Note that the hub cover is the same for both types.

rear differential cover plate and a drain plug on the lowest point of the centre banjo. The rear axle was always finished in black, with the nosepiece in natural aluminium. Axles were individually numbered but these numbers were not entered in the production records. The number, with up to five figures, was stamped on the front of the left-hand rear axle tube.

REAR SUSPENSION

Conventional semi-elliptic leaf springs were employed, with six leaves (including the master leaf) and a bottom plate, fitted below the axle and secured with U bolts. There was no interleaving between the spring leaves. Bump rubbers and rebound straps were fitted to control the extremes of axle movement. Armstrong lever arm shock absorbers, in natural aluminium with arms painted black, were fitted inside the chassis frame side members in front of the axle.

In 1959, Twin Cam models could be fitted with higher setting shock absorber hydraulic valves (front and rear), if required for competition. Otherwise the rear suspension, springs and shock absorbers were the same on all models, and were not subject to any changes during the production run.

Individual spring leaves were $^{7}/_{32}$in gauge and $1^{3}/_{4}$in wide. The free length of the springs was $42^{1}/_{2}$in (+0/-$^{1}/_{8}$in). The distance between the spring eyes was $42^{3}/_{16}$in (free), $42^{1}/_{2}$in (at working load of 450lbs). Free camber was 3.6in, camber at working load 0.

The adjustable steering column seen here was optional on all models.

STEERING

The rack-and-pinion steering, supplied by Cam Gears, was broadly identical on all models, but because the steering rack was positioned slightly further forward on the Twin Cam and De Luxe models, these cars had a longer steering pinion and a different rack housing assembly. All cars incorporated a Hardy Spicer universal joint in the steering column. The lower part of the steering column below this joint was slightly angled towards the centre of the car. The upper part was held in place by two mounting brackets, under the chassis goalpost and under the scuttle respectively. The steering rack housing and column were painted black.

A steering column with telescopic adjustment was available as an optional extra on all models. It had a bolt-on clamp and a chrome-plated telescopic finisher. Late 1600 Mark II cars supplied to Sweden and Germany were fitted with a combined steering column and ignition lock which also activated the starter. This lock was made by Neiman and was introduced in production in May 1961. Two different types may be found. The steering lock was always fitted in conjunction with an adjustable steering column.

The steering wheel, supplied by Wilmot Breeden, was a unique design, with four triple-wire spokes set in a low X-formation, With the front wheels in the straight ahead position, the X should be horizontal. The steering wheel covering and the hub were black. The hub had a plastic cover with a chrome-plated ring and an MG badge in the centre. The badge surround was chrome, with a white background inside the octagon, and chrome letters. The steering wheel was 16½in (419mm) in diameter.

A wood-rim light alloy steering wheel could be specified as an optional extra from December 1957. Described as 'Italian-style', it was supplied by Bluemels (type SW/544, BMC part number AHH5800-Y). It had three spokes in T-formation, with long slots in each spoke. The hub was rivetted and incorporated the standard steering wheel centre.

The steering ratio was 13.5:1, with 2⅔ turns lock to lock. The turning circle was 30ft 6in (9.3m) on 1500 models, in excess of 32ft (9.8m) on Twin Cam and De Luxe models, and 28ft (8.5m) on 1600 and Mark II models.

On early 1500 models, very slender steering arms were fitted, and these are not interchangeable with parts from later models. Service Memorandum MG/356 issued in March 1961 stated that maintenance-free nylon ball joints were progressively being introduced for the steering side levers and cross rods, and they are also mentioned in the Workshop Manual, but there is no information about a specific change point. Otherwise there were no important modifications to the steering during the production run.

FRONT SUSPENSION

The well-proven independent front suspension design from the TD and TF models was carried over on the MGA. It featured double wishbones and coil springs, with the shock absorber arms forming the upper wishbones. The main differences between the various models concerned the steering knuckles and hubs, which were of different types on the 1500, Twin Cam/De Luxe and 1600 models to allow for the three different types of front brakes. Wire wheeled cars also had different hubs from disc wheeled cars.

On the 1500 model, from car/chassis 15152, new front coil springs were introduced. They were made from thicker-gauge wire and had a reduced free length to stiffen up the front suspension, and were only interchangeable in pairs. The steering knuckles and nuts were modified from car/chassis 54247 with washers being added. From car/chassis 66574, the spring pans were modified to permit the installation of an anti-roll bar, and cars equipped with this also had altered lower wishbones. These two modifications were introduced on all Twin Cam models from car/chassis 2275 and the anti-roll bar was fitted as standard on the Twin Cam from then on. The De Luxe model also had the anti-roll bar as standard, but it remained an option on the standard 1600 and 1600 Mark II models. Slightly modified front hubs, with bolts rather than studs for the front brake discs, were introduced on 1600 models from car/chassis 69505 (disc wheeled cars) and 70276 (wire wheeled cars).

Front suspension data was as follows, for all models: camber angle, 1° positive to ½° negative; castor angle, 4°; king pin inclination, 9° to 10½°; toe-in, nil (wheels parallel).

The same type of Armstrong double-acting lever arm piston type shock absorber was found on all models. They were in natural aluminium, with the arms painted black. Additional competition shock absorbers, Andrex friction type TE.1, could be fitted to the front suspension with special mounting brackets. They were available for all models except the 1600 Mark II, but should not be fitted in conjunction with the anti-roll bar. The Twin Cam could be fitted with higher setting hydraulic valves to front (and rear) shock absorbers which was recommended for circuit racing. It is uncertain when this modification became available, but it was probably in January 1959.

BRAKES

No fewer than three different braking systems were found on MGA cars. This section will deal first with the Lockheed all-drum system found on 1500 model, then (to preserve the chronological order) with the Dunlop all-disc system of the Twin Cam and

The front brake drum of the 1500 model.

The Lockheed disc brake fitted to the front of the 1600 and Mark II models.

De Luxe models, and finally with the Lockheed front disc/rear drum system of the 1600 and 1600 Mark II models.

On the 1500, the drums were 10in in diameter and $1\frac{3}{4}$in wide at front and rear. The front brakes had two wheel cylinders and thus two leading shoes, but the rear brakes had one wheel cylinder and a leading and a trailing shoe. Ferodo DM13 linings, size 9.6in × 1.75in, gave a total lining area of 67.2 sq in at both front and rear. The drums were painted black. There was a combined brake and clutch hydraulic master cylinder with integral supply tank positioned on the horizontal shelf behind the engine above the footwell. The master cylinder was left as an unpainted casting with the supply tank cover in natural metal finish.

The pendant pedals were directly below the master cylinder, the pedal arms passing through a complicated one-piece black rubber fume excluder (which was different on Twin Cam and De Luxe models). The pedals had shield-shaped pads with vertical grooves. Pedal design was modified at car/chassis 58713. At car/chassis 27989 (disc wheeled cars) and 28540 (wire wheeled cars), the three-way connection and brake

The Dunlop disc brake found on the front of Twin Cam and De Luxe models. On this Twin Cam, the front inner wing has been split, which is not original.

The rear disc brake of the Twin Cam and De Luxe models.

pipes to the rear brakes were modified to incorporate standardized UNF threads. At car/chassis 22741, the banjo connection to the rear wheel brake cylinders was changed from a straight to a right-angle type.

The handbrake, of the fly-off type, was fitted on the right-hand side of the propeller shaft tunnel, being conveniently horizontal and out of the way in the off position. It activated the rear brakes by cable. The lever was chrome-plated with a plain black handgrip without finger holds. The setting button was also chrome-plated.

The Dunlop disc brakes fitted to the Twin Cam and De Luxe models were of 11in diameter. These cars had separate brake and clutch master cylinders, and the brake pipe runs were somewhat different compared to ordinary MGAs. The disc brake calipers were modified at approximately car/chassis 836, and at car/chassis 997 the master cylinder box was modified to avoid the fitting of a taper packing between master cylinder and box. The use of Wakefield Crimson brake fluid (later Dunlop disc brake fluid) was recommended, or alternatively another brake fluid to specification SAE70.R1 or SAE70.R3.

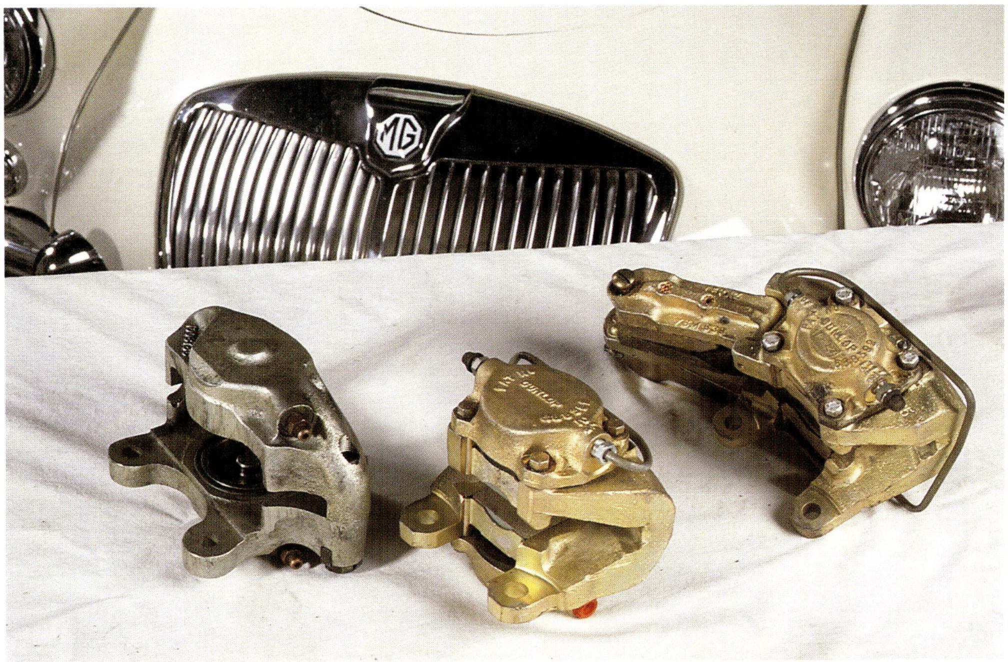

Three disc brake calipers: the Lockheed type found on the 1600 and Mark II models (left), the front caliper from the Twin Cam and De Luxe models (centre), and the rear caliper from these cars (right) with the additional carrier for the handbrake pads.

The master cylinder box, with separate reservoirs for brakes and clutch, in situ on a Twin Cam.

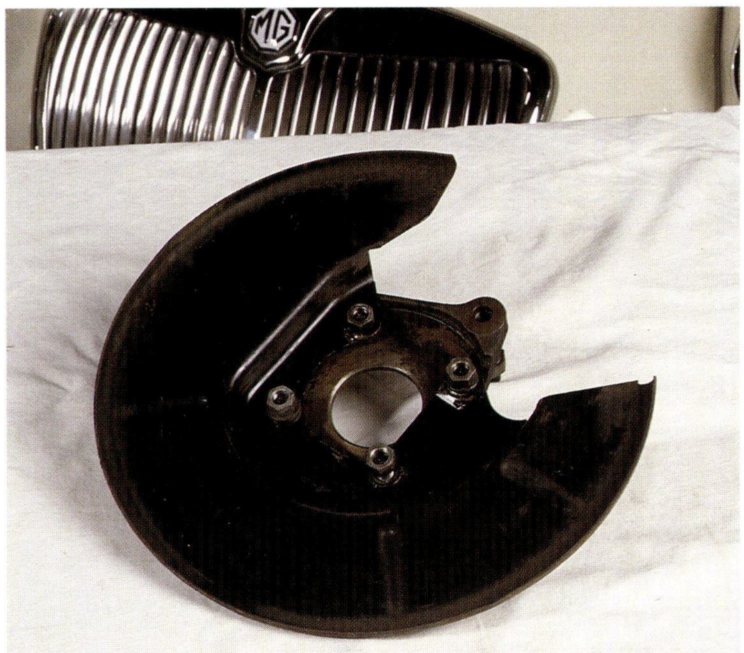

This dust cover was added to the 1600 Mark II front disc brakes in July 1961, but can also be retro-fitted on earlier models.

The handbrake mechanism was like the 1500 as far as the lever and cable were concerned, but the handbrake operated on special pad carriers attached to the rear brake disc calipers. These were not terribly effective and were troublesome to set up – yet another of the Twin Cam's little bugbears. The De Luxe models used a slightly modified Twin Cam type master cylinder, and a service kit was made available to convert a Twin Cam master cylinder to the latest specification.

On the 1600 and 1600 Mark II models (other than De Luxe models), 11in Lockheed disc brakes were fitted on the front wheels and 10in drum brakes on the rear wheels. The studs for fitting the brake discs to the front hubs were replaced by bolts at car/chassis 69505 (disc wheeled cars) and 70276 (wire wheeled cars). At car/chassis 78106, improved brake pads were introduced, and the new type was recommended for all replacements on earlier cars. On the 1600 Mark II model, dust covers for the brake discs were introduced from car/chassis 102589. The rear drum brakes on all 1600 and 1600 Mark II models were the same as on the 1500 model, although new DON24 linings were specified, size 9.63 × 1.7in.

In the foreground is the accelerator pedal for a right-hand drive car. At the back is the cross shaft and pedal from a left-hand drive car which enables the passenger to operate the accelerator unawares (or not!).

Whereas an earlier photo showed the handbrake in the off position, here it is in the on position, with the gearlever also seen in detail.

From the start of 1600 production, the brake pedal arm was changed in shape, and the master cylinder was fitted with a much deeper cover for the supply tank. The hydraulic pipe runs and the handbrake mechanism were largely as on the 1500 model, and were not subject to any modifications during the 1600 and 1600 Mark II production run.

WHEELS & TYRES

The standard road wheel was a bolt-on steel disc wheel, made by Dunlop, size 4J×15, with four-stud fixing and twelve round ventilation holes. From 1500 car/chassis 52070, the wheels were strengthened and made more crack resistant by a slight modification adjacent to the brake adjuster holes, but there was no change to the part number (ACH 8004). From 1500 car/chassis 63577, lighter but stronger wheels were introduced under a new part number (AHH 8010). The gauge of the wheel centre was increased from 10 SWG (.128in) to 9 SWG (.144in), while the thickness of the rim was decreased from 13 SWG (.092in) to 14 SWG (.080in). Weight was down from almost 17lbs to 15lbs. The new wheels were of a slightly altered appearance, with more oval ventilation holes, and were recommended as replacements for earlier cars. They were used until the end of production in 1962. These later wheels also had increased curvature to the section of the wheel centre,

A variety of disc-type MGA wheels. The two on the left are the Twin Cam type, seen from both sides and in primer finish. The two on the right are different types of bolt-on wheels, the early 1500 type (without a tyre) and the later 1500 type which was also fitted to all 1600 models (with a non-original radial). The tyre in the background is much more interesting, being a whitewall version of the Dunlop Road Speed RS5 tyre which could be fitted to 1600 and Mark II models.

There is very little visual difference, but this is the later-style disc wheel which is necessary on models with front disc brakes to clear the calipers. The hub caps are of this simple design, and never had an MG medallion in the centre.

giving sufficient clearance for the disc brake calipers on the 1600 and Mark II models.

The disc wheels were fitted with plain hub caps, lacking the MG badge, except possibly on some early cars according to 1955 photos and brochures. Pre-production MGAs may well have used TF or Magnette ZA style hub caps. Two types of hub caps were found, either made of 22 SWG EN2A mild steel and chrome-plated, or of 26 SWG EN60 stainless steel – but they were identical in appearance.

Chrome-plated Ace rimbellishers could be fitted as optional extras but were discontinued at car/chassis 63576 and do not fit the later type wheel. A modified rimbellisher suitable for the later wheel was available only as a dealer-fitted accessory. Full-diameter Ace Mercury wheel discs were also available as options. According to the 1500 Service Parts List, they were discontinued at car/chassis 63576 but reappeared in modified form on the 1600 model from car/chassis 68851. The later Ace Mercury wheel discs would also fit a late-model 1500 with the new type wheel.

Of these wire wheels, the normal 48-spoke type is fitted on the car. The two 60-spoke competition type wheels in the foreground show the steel rim (left) and the aluminium rim (right).

The knock-ons on the left are for pushrod cars, with the early type (bearing the MG logo) above the later type (shared with Austin-Healeys). The two on the right are the coarser-threaded varieties used on the Twin Cam – the earlier steel type is above the later bronze type.

The wheels were usually painted aluminium – probably BMC colour code AL.1 – but it appears that early 1500 models could have the wheels finished in body colour, if the optional rimbellishers were specified as a factory fitment.

Dunlop 48-spoke wire wheels, size 4J×15, with steel rims and centre-lock fixing, were available as optional equipment. They had 16 long outer spokes and 32 short inner spokes. They were usually fixed with knock-ons, originally featuring the MG badge in the centre, the words 'right (off) side' or 'left (near) side', and 'undo' with an arrow in the appropriate direction. The knock-ons were changed twice during the 1500 production run, at car/chassis 40857 to have a more curved section across the centre of the knock-on, and again at 48730, the last type not having the MG badge. In October 1958, somewhere around car/chassis 57500, octagonal spinners were introduced on cars for Germany and were subsequently also fitted for the Swiss market. They never had the MG badge. Not available as original factory-fitted equipment, but quoted as part of the racing and competition equipment, were 60-spoke wire wheels, size 4½×15, with either steel or aluminium rims. The wire wheels were painted aluminium; it does not appear that chrome-plated wire wheels were ever available.

The final type of wheel which may be found on an MGA is the centre-lock disc wheel, also made by Dunlop, used for the Twin Cam and De Luxe models. These wheels featured 15 ventilation holes, were made from steel and had peg drive to the hubs. Neither the wheel hubs nor the knock-ons of the Twin Cam and De Luxe models were interchangeable with those of an ordinary MGA of any model. The Twin Cam knock-ons had a coarser thread than those found on pushrod cars. The knock-ons were modified at Twin Cam car/chassis 1826, the material changing from steel to bronze, while Twin Cams for Germany had octagonal spinners from car/chassis 708. These octagonal spinners and the later type knock-on were carried over on the De Luxe model. A few early Twin Cams may have had black wheels, but these wheels were normally painted aluminium.

Original tyres on all MGAs were Dunlop cross-plies, with the proviso that some export cars (fully assembled or CKD) were

Taken from the driver's footwell, this shot shows the underside of the heater and the various pipe and wire runs to the central part of the facia.

The heater in close up. The car featured is again the 1600 Mark II De Luxe left-hand drive roadster, which explains some of the detail variations seen here.

shipped from the factory without tyres and tubes and could have been fitted with locally-supplied tyre equipment of other makes in their countries of destination. Standard tyres were size 5.60-15, fitted with tubes. Tubeless tyres could be fitted on disc-wheeled cars, and were often found on pushrod cars, especially for the USA. Reinforced six-ply tyres were fitted on cars for the African continent. Whitewall tyres were a popular option, especially in the USA. Dunlop Road Speed (RS4) tyres, size 5.90-15, were an option from the start of production and were always fitted with inner tubes. One early 1500 sales brochure quotes their size as 5.50-15. They were standard on the Twin Cam model.

On the 1600 models, the same tyre options were available, but during the 1600 production run the Road Speed tyres were updated to the RS5 type, which was fitted to all De Luxe models. A whitewall version of the Road Speed tyre became available. On the 1600 Mark II model, from car/chassis 103192, the latest type of Dunlop Gold Seal nylon tyres in black or whitewall versions were introduced as standard equipment, except for cars exported to Germany which by then had Road Speed tyres as standard.

Nowadays, many cars will be fitted with radial ply tyres, typically size 155-15 or 165-15. These are likely to bring benefits in terms of handling, steering accuracy and longevity, at the price of additional road noise, a slightly harsher ride, and possibly somewhat heavier steering.

ELECTRICAL EQUIPMENT & LAMPS

On all models, the Lucas 12 volt electrical system with positive earth connection had two 6 volt batteries connected in series. The batteries were mounted in cradles on the chassis frame behind the seats, and were accessible when the floor of the hood stowage compartment was lifted. The original type of battery was SG9E, except on certain export cars which were supplied with dry-charged batteries type STGZ9E. Each battery was held in place by a strip of angle iron and two rods which were threaded at the top for double lock nuts and hooked at the bottom, fitting into holes in the cradle frame. Some export cars, whether fully assembled or CKD, were shipped less batteries. Cars supplied for police use could be fitted with

This is an unusual view of the area behind the facia of a left-hand drive MGA – a 1600 Mark II De Luxe roadster. We are looking upwards and towards the left from the passenger footwell. The steering column is at the bottom of the picture. The demister hoses from the heater occupy the middle ground, with one of the facia support brackets at the top.

larger batteries (type SFF17E-6 or later SFLY17E-6) which required larger battery cradles and therefore a slightly modified chassis. Battery covers became available as optional extras from April 1959, but could also be fitted to earlier cars.

The original type of dynamo was C39PV-2 (Lucas part number 22258) with a modification occurring early in the 1500 production run from engine number 15GB/487 when the so-called windowless yoke dynamo (without brush gear inspection windows) was introduced. On the 1600 model, from engine number 16GA/6272, a dynamo type C40-1 (part number 22700) or alternatively type C40 (part number 22704) was fitted. Police cars were usually fitted with a high-output dynamo, originally type C45PV-6 (part number 22483 or 22530), but from car/chassis 101840 1600 Mark II police cars were fitted with a type C42 (part number 22902) which required a ½in wide fan belt and different pulleys. The Twin Cam dynamo was also a type C39PV-2 but was modified for this application and had Lucas part number 22295. All dynamos were originally painted red to match the engine colour, but some replacements were black.

A starter motor type M35G-1 (part number 25022) was fitted to all models, although a change occurred to the commutator end bracket and the brush tension springs in February 1961, and on 1600 Mark II models from engine number 16GC/6435 the starter motor internals were redesigned. The revised starter motor was listed as type M35 (under part number 25079) and was interchangeable with the original design. Starter motors were mostly painted engine red but could also be black. It is worth remembering that although the position of the starter motor had been raised at car/chassis 61504, the point of introduction of the 15GD type engine on the 1500 model, the starter motor itself was not changed, although a rubber cover was fitted between the gearbox tunnel and the right-hand toeboard to protect the exposed Bendix spring. This cover was also found on the Twin Cam and all 1600 models.

The control box was type RB106-2 (part number 37182) on most models, including the Twin Cam. It was modified on the 1600 model when Lucar snap connectors were introduced for the dynamo harness from engine number 16GA/6272, probably coinciding with car/chassis 74489 when the main harness was also modified. In approximately January 1961 (possibly earlier), the carbon composite type resistance in the control box was replaced by the improved wire-wound type, the part number becoming 37183. Police cars had a control box type RB310 (originally possibly part number 37189, later 37297), but from car/chassis 101840 the police car control box became type RB340 (part number 37331) to suit the C42 dynamo. On right-hand drive cars, the control box was found on the left-hand side of the bulkhead, and on left-hand drive cars it was on the right-hand side. All cars had a separate fuse box type SF6, with two 35amp fuses and two spares.

Most MGA cars had headlamps of type F700 Mark VI, with certain exceptions detailed below. Many cars have been fitted with the P700 lamps with the distinctive tripod, but these were never originally quoted for any MGA. However, there were several different versions according to the destinations of individual cars, as follows:

- All home market cars, right-hand drive export cars in general and cars for Sweden (until 1600 car/chassis 72039 and Twin Cam car/chassis 2417): dip left, standard lens (Lucas part number 51344). From car/chassis 105362, these lamps were fitted with a new integral skirted gasket and dust excluder and the Lucas part number became 58850.

- Cars for Sweden from 1600 car/chassis 72040 and Twin Cam car/chassis 2418: dip left, asymmetrical European lens (Lucas part number 58451).

- Left-hand drive cars for non-European export markets except USA (but including Canada until 1600 Mark II car/chassis 107030): dip right, standard lens (Lucas part number 51345, for Canada number 51533). This type of headlamp was modified at car/chassis 105362 to incorporate the combined skirted gasket and dust excluder.

- Left-hand drive cars for European markets, except France and Sweden, until 1500 car/chassis 58917 and Twin Cam car/chassis 823: vertical dip, standard lens (Lucas part number 51346). From 1500 car/chassis 58918 and Twin Cam car/chassis 824, these lamps were fitted with the new asymmetrical lenses and the Lucas part number became 58272.

- Left-hand drive cars for France and certain French overseas territories differed from the general European type in being fitted with yellow bulbs. They were originally Lucas part number 51411, but the asymmetrical lenses were introduced from 1500 car/chassis 60340 and Twin Cam car/chassis 1618, and the Lucas part number was changed to 58273.

- Cars for the USA were originally shipped with Mark VI headlamps without light units (Lucas part number 51467) but with Ward and Goldstone adaptors for sealed beam units – typically made by GEC – to be installed locally, complying with US legislation. USA-bound cars left the factory with a protective mask over the headlamp light unit aperture. However, from 1600 car/chassis 70222 and Twin Cam car/chassis 2278, US cars were fitted with Lucas SB700 Mark VIII headlamps incorporating sealed beam units (Lucas part number 58499) from the factory. On 1600 Mark II cars from car/chassis 102857, SB700 Mark X sealed beam headlamps were fitted, and these headlamps were also fitted on cars for Canada from car/chassis 107031 (Lucas part number 58621).

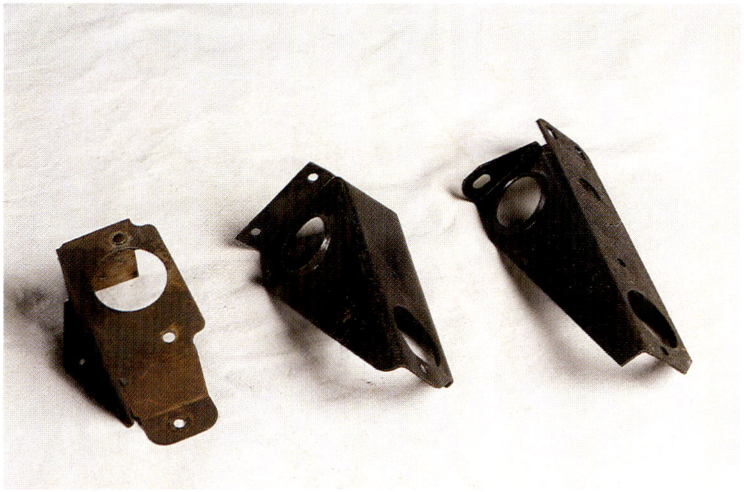

The dipswitch bracket on the left is from a left-hand drive car made from January 1959 onwards – this type screws to the toeboard. The bracket in the centre is from an earlier 1500 car, with either right-hand or left-hand drive, and is suspended from the bulkhead above the footwell. The bracket on the right is from a right-hand drive car made after January 1959.

A foot-operated dipswitch was fitted to the left of the clutch pedal on all cars. On left-hand drive cars, the dip switch bracket was modified and repositioned for easier operation from the start of the 1600 model, and from Twin Cam car/chassis 2281.

The sidelamps which incorporated the front flashing indicators were originally type 539 (Lucas part number 52236) with all-white lenses and a single bulb. These were found on all 1500 models, and on Twin Cams until car/chassis 2192. On Twin Cams from car/chassis 2193 and on all 1600 models, the larger type 632 lamps were fitted (part number 52425), with separate bulbs for the sidelamps and for the flashers. The lenses for these lamps had four triangular lugs or ears in diagonal cross formation around the edge. On home market and many export cars the upper (indicator) part of the lens was amber, the lower (sidelamp) part white, but on left-hand drive cars for the USA, Canada, Italy and Switzerland the lenses were all white. The all-white lamp was Lucas type 630, part number 52430.

The original type of stop/tail lamp with built-in reflector was type 549 (Lucas part number 53330), found on the 1500, Twin Cam and 1600 (Mark I) models. On the 1500 models, and on the Twin Cam until car/chassis 2192, these lamps were also used as flashing indicators, but the later Twin Cams and the 1600 (Mark I) models had separate rear flashers, mounted together with the stop/tail lamps on new plinths. The separate rear flashers were type 594, either with amber lenses (Lucas part number 52337) found on home market and many export cars, or with red lenses (Lucas part

The typical Lucas F700 headlamp fitted to most cars except those for North America, with the larger sidelamp fitted from the start of 1600 production, here with the amber lens for the flashing indicator. The little ears on the front of this type of sidelamp lens were originally more triangular in shape but seem to have been changed some time during the MGA production run.

The small sidelamp fitted on 1500 models and early Twin Cams.

number 53600) found on cars for the USA and Canada.

On the 1600 Mark II, totally new rear lamp units were fitted, installed on horizontal plinths on the rear panel below the boot lid. These were type 647 and were similar to those found on Austin/Morris Mini Mark I cars (1959-67). In these units, the stop/tail lamp, reflector and flashing indicator were combined in one assembly, with two bulbs. The indicator part of the lens could again be amber or red, depending on market. These lamps were handed (not the same on both sides).

A flasher unit type FL5 (alternatively type FL3) was fitted on the bulkhead, but only the 1500 and early Twin Cam models had the flasher relay type DB10 which was rendered superfluous on later cars with the separate flashing indicator lamps. The flasher relay was mounted to the left of the flasher unit.

The number plate lamp on most cars was type 467, originally with a single 4 watt bulb (Lucas part no. 53093), but two 4 watt bulbs were fitted from 1600 car/chassis 88844. The two-bulb lamp type is sometimes known as 467-2 and had Lucas part number 53836. The only exception concerned cars for Switzerland, which had a different number plate lamp, type 469 (Lucas part number 53905), from 1600 car/chassis 92679. This bigger lamp had two 6 watt bulbs and was much like that fitted, for instance, to the Rover P4 range, but did not incorporate a reversing lamp. On the MGA it was fitted on a special bracket. All number plate lamps had chrome-plated shells.

A Lucas SFT576 fog lamp with chrome-plated shell (Lucas part 55128) could be specified as an optional extra, normally to be mounted on the nearside (kerb side) of the car, but on cars for the USA and later France, if a fog lamp was required two lamps were fitted due to local regulations, and two lamps could be ordered also for other

The original rear lamp and small plinth, found on the 1500 and early Twin Cam, with a black gasket between plinth and wing.

The 1600-type rear lamp and separate flashing indicator on the larger plinth, with a grey gasket. The rear lamp lens should be fixed with crosshead screws, and this indicator lens appears to be an incorrect later plastic type – it should be glass.

The combined rear lamp and indicator of the 1600 Mark II.

markets. If two lamps were fitted, an additional relay type SB40-1 was required.

Only a single horn, Lucas Windtone type WT618-L (part number 69046), was fitted as standard, mounted on the inside of the right-hand chassis front extension, below the radiator duct valance panel. An additional high note horn (type WT618-H, Lucas part number 69047) could be supplied as an optional extra, being mounted in the same location on the opposite side of the chassis. Horns were painted black.

The wiper motor was type DA48 on right-hand drive cars, type DA49 on left-hand drive cars, later quoted as type DR2 on all cars. The Lucas part number was 75297 throughout. The motor was mounted on the left-hand side of the horizontal shelf behind the engine, under the bonnet surround shroud, on both right-hand and left-hand drive cars. At least from 1500 car/chassis 12800 (left-hand drive) and 13612 (right-hand drive) – and probably also on earlier cars – 9½in chrome-plated wiper arms were fitted, with 8in blades. The wiper arms had a 15° crank and the angle of the swept area was 120°. The wipers were self-parking and were so arranged that they always parked on the driver's side of the car, on both right-hand and left-hand drive cars. The wiper spindles on the scuttle were chrome-plated. The wiper wheelbox assemblies were changed at 1600 car/chassis 80384, Twin Cam car/chassis 2545.

On early 1500 models, possibly until 1958, individual wires were cloth covered, and the outer braiding for the wiring harness was black with a six-ply white cross pattern. On later cars, individual wires were PVC insulated and plastic covered, and the harness braiding had a yellow tracer on pushrod cars, white on the Twin Cam. The headlamp wires were always cloth covered. The facia wiring loom cover had a brown tracer with a white cross. Some late Mark II cars had a grey rather than black harness cover. The

The rear number plate backing plate at the top is the short, deep type fitted to cars for export to North America. Below is the combined bracket for number plate backing plate and lamp found on all other cars.

covers for individual wires were always colour-coded according to the normal Lucas system.

On 1600 Mark II cars for Germany or Sweden fitted with the combined steering and ignition lock and key-operated starter, a separate starter solenoid switch was fitted on the right-hand wheelarch in the engine compartment.

EXPORT VARIATIONS

Most of the export variations have been described in detail in the individual sections of this book, but the following summary may be useful to readers in individual countries:

North American cars (USA) Left-hand drive, miles-per-hour speedometer, Fahrenheit temperature gauge, sealed beam headlamp units fitted locally (from June 1959, factory fitted), white front and red rear indicator lenses (1600 and later models from May 1959), differently shaped rear number plate backing plate, fog lamps (optional extra) fitted in pairs (from August 1958).

North American cars (Canada) As for the USA, but headlamps always fitted in factory and sealed beam units only fitted from February 1962.

European cars in general Left-hand drive, kilometres speedometer, Centigrade temperature gauge from October 1958, vertical dip headlamps (with asymmetrical lenses from November 1958), amber front and rear indicator lenses (1600 and later models from May 1959).

The following countries required exceptions to general European specification:

Sweden Headlamps dipping to the left, asymmetrical lenses from July 1959, steering column lock including ignition lock and key-operated starter from May 1961. Cars for Sweden normally had left-hand drive.

Germany Wire wheel cars (and Twin Cam/De Luxe models) with octagonal spinners from October 1958, special car/chassis number plate from June 1961, steering column lock (as Swedish cars) from July 1961, later cars fitted Road Speed tyres as standard (at least from August 1961).

France Headlamps fitted with yellow bulbs, asymmetrical lenses from December 1958, special framed safety rear view mirror (Wingard PP.2420) from November 1959, fog lamps fitted only in pairs (when fitted) from February 1961.

Switzerland White front indicator lenses on 1600 and later models from May 1959, special number plate lamp from May 1960, twin silencer exhaust system from December 1961. From April 1961, Swiss cars were also fitted with octagonal spinners on wire wheels or centre-lock disc wheels. Some Swiss customers still requested right-hand drive cars for driving on mountain roads. Some cars may have been shipped to Switzerland without batteries.

This is the centigrade water temperature gauge found on left-hand drive cars for European markets from October 1958.

Italy White front indicator lenses from May 1959 on 1600 and later models.

Other smaller variations found on specific export models included:

Cars for the **African continent** were fitted with six-ply tyres.

North American cars delivered to **Germany** with wire wheels or centre-lock disc wheels had octagonal spinners from October 1958 (and sometimes kilometres speedometers).

Cars for **Mexico** were more or less to North American specification but had kilometres speedometers, and Centigrade temperature gauges (from October 1958).

The most important differences to the various CKD specifications were as follows:

Australia CKD kits were shipped less tyres, tubes, batteries, rear springs, ignition coil, spark plugs, hood material, spare wheel cover, all soft trim, all carpets, door pads and linings, all timber and floorboards, seats. The following parts were included: hood frame, hood rear window and quarterlights, seat frames, seat slides and Dunlopillo cushions. All cars had wire wheels and the standard rear axle ratio. A heater was not normally fitted.

South Africa CKD kits were shipped less tyres, tubes, batteries, windscreen glass, tyre levers and tyre valve spanner. They were supplied with seats, trim and hood, and had a tonneau cover as standard. Piping for wings and radiator grille was black. Both roadsters and coupés were shipped. A heater was not normally fitted.

Eire CKD kits were shipped less tyres, tubes, spark plugs, windscreen glass, rear springs and tyre valve spanner. The rear spring bolts, bushes and clips were supplied. A licence disc holder was supplied.

Mexico CKD kits were shipped less tyres, tubes, batteries, tyre levers and tyre valve spanner. Cars had wire wheels as standard. Trim was fully assembled. The 4.55:1 rear axle was usually fitted, and coupés were shipped as well as roadsters.

Netherlands CKD kits were shipped less tyres, tubes, batteries, windscreen glass, tyre levers and tyre valve spanner. Cars could have either disc or wire wheels. Soft trim was supplied fully assembled.

Finally, two notes must be made as far as the 1600 Mark II model is concerned. Export cars were fitted with the low compression (8.3:1) engine, except cars for the USA and Canada. Export cars had the oil cooler as standard from car/chassis 102737 (coupé) or 102950 (roadster).

PRODUCTION CHANGES BY CAR/CHASSIS NUMBERS

(See also separate list for production changes by engine numbers)

MGA 1500

10101 (May 55)
First MGA 1500.

10501 (Nov 55)
Hood frame, canopy and sidescreens modified.

10917 (Dec 55)
Handed hub nuts introduced on rear axle (disc wheel cars).

11450 (Jan 56)
Above modification introduced on wire wheel cars. Rear axle casing modified (wire wheel cars).

11768 (Jan 56)
Banjo deleted from clutch slave cylinder body.

12800 (Mar 56)
9½in wiper arms with 8in blades introduced on left-hand drive cars; this modification introduced on right-hand drive cars from 13612 in Apr 56.

13473 (Apr 56)
Wiring harness, left-hand headlamp and flasher lead modified.

14090 (Apr 56)
New style instruments introduced.

15152 (May 56)
New coil springs with reduced free length.

16101 (Jun 56)
Vynide hood modified, seams capped and welded after stitching.

17220 (Jul 56)
Facia panel piping modified.

17588 (Jul 56)
Speedometer and rev counter cables modified.

19949 (Sep 56)
Sill finishers added to improve appearance.

20162 (Sep 56)
Rear three-quarter lights added to hood canopy.

20671 (Sep 56)
First coupé.

20753 (Sep 56)
Propeller shaft modified, dust cover added at front.

22741 (Nov 56)
Rear brake wheel cylinders, banjo connection changed from straight to right angle type.

24594 (Dec 56)
Auxiliary return spring fitted to throttle cable.

25110 (Jan 57)
Coupé: external lock fitted to driver's door (previously, this lock was always fitted to the left-hand door).

26681 (Feb 57)
Bonnet lid wood batten modified.

27989 (Mar 57)
Brake piping and rear brake banjo connections, UNF threads standardized on disc wheel cars; this modification introduced on wire wheel cars from 28540 in Apr 57.

29935 (Apr 57)
Splash plates added inside rear wings in front of wheels.

40857 (Oct 57)
Knock-ons changed (from 81614/81615 to ATB 4222/ATB4223).

42613 (Nov 57)
Carburettor distance pieces made from harder material and gaskets added either side.

45186 (Dec 57)
Smaller windscreen washer jets, modified control unit.

48674 (Feb 58)
Time setting for rear shock absorbers reduced to improve ride.

48730 (Feb 58)
Knock-ons changed (from ATB4222/ ATB4223 to 1B8077/1B8078).

48980 (Feb 58)
Roadster: Ash Green colour introduced instead of Tyrolite Green (last Tyrolite Green roadster was 48333).

49000 (Feb 58)
Coupé: Ash Green colour introduced instead of Island Green (last Island Green coupé was 48178).

50270 (Mar 58)
Disc wheels modified in area adjacent to brake adjuster hole.

52916 (Jun 58)
Coupé: door hinges with smaller stops to increase door opening.

54247 (Jul 58)
Front suspension: steering knuckles, levers and nuts modified.

53875 (Jul 58)
Track rod ends: cup and fibre washers added below grease nipples, grease escape drilled in steering ball socket cap on left-hand drive cars; introduced on right-hand drive cars from 55545 in Aug 58.

55633 (Aug 58)
Relay for twin fog lamps fitted on cars for North America.

56069 (Sep 58)
Roadster: door hinges modified (as on coupé from 52916).

57100 (Sep 58)
Windscreen hood pegs changed from plated brass to plated mild steel.

57574 (Oct 58)
Left-hand drive cars (not for North America) fitted with Centigrade temperature gauge instead of Fahrenheit gauge (cp. Twin Cam car number 713). Around this time, octagonal spinners introduced on wire wheel cars for Germany instead of knock-ons.

58713 (Nov 58)
Brake pedal modified. Clutch pedal on left-hand drive cars modified; modified clutch pedal introduced on right-hand drive cars from 61100 in Jan 59.

58918 (Nov 58)
European export cars (except for France and Sweden) fitted with asymmetrical headlamps; rim fixing screw and adaptor modified (cp. Twin Cam car number 824).

58996 (Nov 58)
Front spring spigot increased in diameter to eliminate spring noise (cp. Twin Cam car number 842).

60340 (Dec 58)
Asymmetrical headlamps introduced on cars for France (cp. Twin Cam car number 1618).

60637 (Dec 58)
Tonneau cover fasteners deleted from door tops and tonneau cover zip lengthened on left-hand drive cars; introduced on right-hand drive cars from 64332 in Feb 59 (cp. Twin Cam car number 994). The new tonneau cover did not have a steering wheel bag.

61160 (Jan 59)
Heater water valve of improved design.

61504 (Jan 59)
Introduction of 15GD series engine with high starter position. Gearbox cover with rubber cover for Bendix spring, right-hand toeboard and carpet modified to suit. Left-hand drive cars only: speedometer cable 3in longer to clear starter motor. Gearbox modified. Propeller shaft with splined sliding joint at front, new type propeller shaft found on some cars from 61037.

63435 (Feb 59)
Wiring harness, connections to starter switch and starter motor modified.

63577 (Feb 59)
New disc wheels, stronger but lighter, introduced. Optional rimbellishers discontinued. New type Ace Mercury wheel discs.

66574 (Apr 59)
Chassis front extension and front suspension spring pan assemblies modified to permit installation of optional anti-roll bar (cp. Twin Cam car number 2275).

68850 (May 59)
Last MGA 1500.

MGA 1600

68851 (May 59)
First MGA 1600. New 1588cc engine type 16GA; front disc brakes; half shafts with involute splines, new differential wheels; larger sidelamps/indicators in modified front wings; separate rear indicators and new tail lamp plinths; flasher relay deleted; coupé spare wheel relocated in boot with new rear bulkhead and rear window shelf; new sliding sidescreens, new sidescreen front fixing nut, additional hood catch on windscreen on roadster; new range of colours for paint, trim and hood; new series of body numbers prefixed B (cp. Twin Cam car number 2193).

69505 (Jun 59)
Front disc brakes, studs replaced by bolts on disc wheel cars; introduced on wire wheel cars from 70276.

70222 (Jun 59)
Cars for the USA fitted Mark VIII sealed beam headlamps in the factory with modified headlamp gasket integral with dust excluder (cp. Twin Cam car number 2278).

71832 (Jul 59)
Radiator filler cap changed from 4lb to 7lb to prevent boiling.

72040 (Jul 59)
Cars for Sweden fitted with asymmetrical headlamps (cp. Twin Cam car number 2418).

74489 (Aug 59)
Dynamo wiring harness with Lucar snap connectors introduced, coinciding with engine 16GA/6272; new dynamo and modified control box.

74979 (Sep 59)
Speedometer cable modified on right-hand drive cars (cp. Twin Cam car number 2467).

78106 (Oct 59)
Front disc brake pads of improved material on disc wheel cars; introduced on wire wheel cars from 78114.

78249 (Oct 59)
Hood frame and canopy modified. New sidescreen stowage envelope and modified battery hatch, to enable hood to be stowed under rear tonneau panel, with sidescreens stowed on top of battery hatch rather than in front and improving seat adjustment (cp. Twin Cam car number 2540).

79663 (Nov 59)
Rear view mirror with safety rim fitted on cars for France.

80384 (Nov 59)
Windscreen wiper wheelbox modified (cp. Twin Cam car number 2545).

80390 (Nov 59)
Windscreen washer bottle neck increased in diameter from 1½in to 2³⁄₁₆in, control module modified (cp. Twin Cam car number 2544).

81532 (Dec 59)
Coupé: new type of optional extra sun visor (cp. Twin Cam car number 2061).

82749 (Dec 59)
Half shafts, differential wheels and assembly modified on wire wheel cars; introduced on disc wheel cars from 82893.

88192 (Mar 60)
Radiator filler cap modified.

88844 (Mar 60)
Number plate lamp with two bulbs instead of one bulb.

91240 (Apr 60)
Four-wheel Dunlop disc brakes and centre-lock disc wheels introduced as an option, with sundry other changes – the De Luxe model.

92679 (May 60)
Special number plate lamp on cars for Switzerland.

93225 (May 60)
Rubber cover for fuel pump discontinued.

93548 (Jul 60)
Tool kit reduced, new type of Shelley ratchet jack introduced.

96269 (Aug 60)
Sidescreen rear flap removed and hood valance modified to improve waterproofing, on cars with grey hood/sidescreens. Introduced from 96806 for beige hood/sidescreens, and from 97104 for blue hood/sidescreens.

100351 (Mar 61)
Last MGA 1600 (Mark I).

MGA 1600 MARK II

100352 (Mar 61)
First 1600 Mark II. New 1622cc engine type 16GC; new radiator grille; new combined stop/tail lamps and rear indicators on horizontal plinths below boot lid; 4.1:1 rear axle ratio standard; seat belt mounting points added; facia now covered in Vynide on roadster, scuttle on roadster and coupé covered in Novon.

100596 (Apr 61)
Coupé: on white cars with black trim, piping colour for black facia trim roll changed from white to black. Introduced on roadster from 101490, Jun 61.

100612 (Apr 61)
Fuel pump specification upgraded from AUA 54 to AUA 154.

101353 (May 61)
Rear lamp plinth gasket replaced by cream Prestik.

101292 (May 61)
Roadster: Modified door seal finishers on shut pillars.

101840 (Jun 61)
Police cars: C42 dynamo and RB340 control box introduced. Low compression engine standardized on police cars.

102381 (Jul 61)
Two distance pieces added to rear bumper brackets to bring bumper further away from body, so avoiding risk of rear number plate fouling body.

102589 (Jul 61)
Dust covers added to front disc brakes on standard model with disc wheels; introduced on wire wheel cars from 102929.

102737 (Jul 61)
Oil cooler fitted as standard on export cars (coupé models); on roadster models from 102950 (Aug 61).

102857 (Jul 61)
Headlamps on cars for the USA changed from Mark VIII type to Mark X type.

103030 (Aug 61)
Oil cooler flexible pipes, brass nuts replaced by steel nuts.

103192 (Aug 61)
Nylon tyres introduced as standard, except on cars for Germany.

103261 (Sep 61)
Modified disc brake caliper dust seal on disc wheel cars; introduced on wire wheel cars from 103834.

103759 (Sep 61)
Common type Neiman steering lock fitted to cars for both Germany and Sweden (steering locks fitted to cars for Sweden from May 61, to cars for Germany from 1 July 1961).

104805 (Dec 61)
Exhaust system with twin silencers on cars for Switzerland.

105362 (Dec 61)
Headlamps fitted with skirted gasket with integral dust excluder, separate dust excluder deleted on UK and right-hand drive export cars (and left-hand drive cars not for Europe/USA).

107031 (Feb 62)
USA-type sealed beam headlamps fitted on cars for Canada.

108662 (May 62)
Last coupé.

109070 (May 62)
Last MGA 1600 Mark II.

MGA TWIN CAM

501 (Apr 58)
First MGA Twin Cam.

528 (Jun 58)
Packing plate added to left-hand engine mounting to improve clearance between starting handle dog and steering rack. Air cleaners with positive filter element location.

592 (Sep 58)
Roadster: detachable panels in front wheel arches for improved access; introduced on coupé from 594.

652 (Sep 58)
7lb relief valve added to overflow pipe from radiator header tank; also found on a few earlier cars. Non-pressurised cap fitted to header tank.

708 (Oct 58)
Octagonal spinners on cars for Germany.

713 (Oct 58)
Longer speedometer cable on left-hand drive cars. Centigrade temperature gauge instead of Fahrenheit gauge on left-hand drive cars not for North America (cp. 1500 car number 57574).

824 (Nov 58)
Asymmetrical headlamps introduced on cars for Europe, except for France and Sweden (cp. 1500 car number 58918).

836 (Nov 58)
Modified disc brake caliper units.

842 (Nov 58)
Front spring spigot increased in diameter to eliminate spring noise (cp. 1500 car number 58996).

994 (Dec 58)
Tonneau cover fasteners deleted from door tops and tonneau cover zip lengthened (cp. 1500 car number 60637).

997 (Dec 58)
Brake master cylinder box and strengthening plate modified.

1618 (Mar 59)
Asymmetrical headlamps introduced on cars for France (cp. 1500 car number 60340).

1826 (Apr 59)
Knock-ons of bronze introduced instead of steel knock-ons.

1840 (Apr 59)
Rear hub extensions modified.

2061 (May 59)
Coupé: new type of optional extra sun visor (cp. 1600 car number 81532)

2193 (Jun 59)
Roadster: Introduction of 1600-type body (cp. 1600 car number 68851) with modifications as detailed for MGA 1600. New type of body introduced on coupé from 2292.

2275 (Jun 59)
Chassis front extension, front suspension spring pans and wishbones modified to suit installation of anti-roll bar as standard (cp. 1500 car number 66574).

2278 (Jun 59)
Cars for the USA fitted Mark VIII sealed beam headlamps in factory, with modified headlamp gasket integral with dust excluder (cp. 1600 car number 70222).

2281 (Jun 59)
Dipswitch on left-hand drive cars repositioned for easier operation (this modification introduced on MGA 1600 from start of production).

2371 (Jul 59)
Half shafts with involute splines, differential assembly and wheels modified (introduced on MGA 1600 from start of production).

2418 (Jul 59)
Asymmetrical headlamps introduced on cars for Sweden (cp. 1600 car number 72040).

2467 (Sep 59)
Speedometer cable modified on right-hand drive cars (cp. 1600 car number 74979).

2468 (Sep 59)
Air cleaners modified to incorporate venturi.

2540 (Nov 59)
Hood frame and canopy etc. modified (cp. 1600 car number 78249).

2544 (Nov 59)
Windscreen washer modified (cp. 1600 car number 80390).

2545 (Nov 59)
Windscreen wiper wheelbox modified (cp. 1600 car number 80384).

2611 (May 60)
Last MGA Twin Cam.

On the left, the rimbellisher which was available on the 1500 models until February 1959, with a modified form being available as a dealer-installed accessory on later models. On the right, the Ace Mercury wheel disc, here unfortunately missing the central octagon with the letters MG.

OPTIONS, EXTRAS & ACCESSORIES

The following is a summary of those options or extras which could be specified by the purchaser as factory fitments:

Low rear axle ratio Of 4.555:1 (9/41) with suitable speedometer. Available on all models. See gearbox and rear axle sections.

Wire wheels Not available on Twin Cam or De Luxe models. See section on wheels and tyres.

Whitewall tyres Size 5.60-15, not available on Twin Cam. Road Speed tyres, size 5.90-15: available on 1500, 1600 and 1600 Mark II; standard on Twin Cam and De Luxe. Road Speed whitewall tyres available on 1600 Mark II. Tubeless tyres for disc wheel cars were never a quoted option but were fitted to many cars, particularly pushrod models for the USA. See section on wheels and tyres.

Chrome-plated Ace rimbellishers Available only on 1500 to car/chassis 63576. See section on wheels and tyres. A modified type was subsequently quoted as a dealer-installed accessory on 1600 and Mark II models.

Ace Mercury wheeldiscs Only available on cars with bolt-on disc wheels; not available on Twin Cam or De Luxe models. This was a full-diameter 'turbo' design wheeltrim with an octagonal centre and the letters MG embossed and painted red in the centre. The original type was available on the 1500 model until car/chassis 63576, then a modified type was produced to fit the new type road wheel. See section on wheels and tyres. They are – perhaps deservedly! – rare.

The Ace Mercury wheel disc complete, as fitted to an MGA, can be admired here. Made from aluminium, these wheel discs were fairly flimsy and easily damaged.

Adjustable steering column Available on all models. See steering section.

Luggage carrier This was fitted to the boot lid with two longitudinal 'skis' bolted to the lid with rubber strips for protection. The grid supports, the grid surround, two crossmembers and the rear guard were tubular, and the entire assembly was chrome-plated. It was fitted with chrome-plated domed crosshead screws to the boot lid. When the luggage carrier was fitted, a wing mirror was always fitted on the driver's side (for wing mirror details, see below). The

The Twin Cam heater in close up. From this angle, the remote pressure relief valve in the radiator overflow pipe may also be seen, directly below the vent in the shroud.

Of the two types of radiator blind, this is the one fitted to pushrod cars with the blind pulling upwards from the bottom. The chain, bracket and control are effectively the same also for the Twin Cam version.

This black blanking plate was fitted if the heater was not installed. On this Twin Cam, the original bulkhead wiring loom can also be studied in detail.

luggage carrier was available on all models (and very useful it was too).

Overall tonneau cover Usually in the same colour as the hood. Available on all models. See section on weather equipment.

Radiator blind Supplied by the Key Leather Company. The control (a simple pull chain) was mounted on a bracket behind the facia on the driver's side. Available on all models, but the Twin Cam with its different radiator had a unique radiator blind which pulled sideways across the radiator rather than upwards from the bottom of the radiator.

Heater kit The heater was a Smiths model F.275 of 2¾KW output. The heater unit itself was Smiths number FHR.2453/01 (on pushrod-engined cars) or FHR.2457/01 (Twin Cam). The reason a different heater unit was found on the Twin Cam was that this model had the carburettors and air filters on the right, leaving no space for the heater air intake hose on this side of the car, so the heater unit was a mirror image of the one found on pushrod-engined cars. The heater unit was painted black and was situated on the horizontal shelf behind the engine. It incorporated the heater matrix and blower fan in one unit. The heater air intake hose was of black paper foil laminate on pushrod

One of several types of standard Radiomobile radio – type 40T long and medium wave.

cars, and of rubber reinforced with wire on the Twin Cam, and stretched forward past the engine and radiator. The heater controls are described in the section dealing with the facia and instruments. The heater was by far the most common MGA option and was available on all models. It was, however, still not fitted to a substantial number of home market cars, and was usually omitted on cars supplied to hot climates, including Australia and South Africa but also some parts of the USA. If the heater was not fitted, the hole in the bulkhead shelf was covered by a black cover plate.

Additional high-note horn Lucas WT618-H, see section on electrical equipment. Available on all models.

Fog lamp Lucas SFT576. Mounted on a bracket behind the front bumper overrider, usually on the nearside of the car. Two fog lamps could be supplied, and in certain markets (USA, France) fog lamps were later only fitted in pairs, requiring an extra relay. See section on electrical equipment. Available on all models.

HMV Radiomobile car radio With loudspeaker and aerial. Several different types of radio were available, as follows:

Long and medium wave push-button types 200XA, 200R, 400TA, 500TA or 600T

Long and medium wave non-push button types 220XE, 20X, 40T or 50T

Medium wave push-button types 402TA, 502TA or 602T

This is Radiomobile's later type 50T radio, with black controls, a chrome-plated finisher and a different scale. It is shown together with the loudspeaker and its mounting brackets.

Medium wave non-push button types 42T or 52T

Medium and short wave low output type 230RA

Medium and short wave high output type 230RB

The radio control unit was mounted in the aperture on the facia, with the loudspeaker on a bracket behind the grille and the amplifier/tuner on brackets below the scuttle. The aerial was the retractable type, mounted on the kerbside front wing. Available on all models. Types 200XA, 200R, 220XE and 20X were quoted on early 1500 models. Types 400TA, 40T, 402TA and 42T were quoted for the 1500 model from late 1958; 500TA, 50T, 502TA and 52T for the 1600 and Twin Cam; while on 1600 Mark II models, types 600T and 602T were quoted together with types 50T and 52T.

With the rakish competition windscreen, the grab handles of the standard windscreen and the wipers were omitted.

The short wave receiving types were the same for all models. There may well have been some overlap in the radio types between different models, and other types could have been available on early 1500 models. The push-button long and medium wave was the 'standard' type fitted, unless the purchaser specified another type.

Competition windscreen This was a perspex windscreen originally mounted in a chrome-plated brass frame, later in an aluminium frame, and was made by Auster. Two or three different heights were found around 6 to 8in. It was raked further back than the standard windscreen and grab handles were not fitted to the frame. If the competition windscreen was fitted, wipers and windscreen washer were omitted. It was a very unusual option indeed. Available on all models.

Wing mirror One or two, Lucas 406, Wingard 1C or (from January 1961) a Desmo Boomerang mirror with convex glass. Available on all models. If the luggage carrier was fitted, a wing mirror on the driver's side was always supplied as well.

Cold air ventilation kit Smiths number FHQ.6298/02 (pushrod-engined cars) or FHQ.6298/03 (Twin Cam). Fitted as an alternative to the heater, predominantly on cars for hot climates. May be simply described as a heater without the heat exchange matrix. Available on all models.

Smokers welcome here. The optional cigar lighter and one of two types of ash tray. The other type, more common, had a wider bottom flange with four screw holes. The type seen here may only be correct for early 1500 models. Regrettably, the Swan Vestas box is not the contemporary original type for an MGA.

Hard top Two distinct types of hard top were available. The original type, made by BMC subsidiary Vanden Plas, was in aluminium and was painted black. It featured a wrap-around rear window which appeared to be divided in three sections, but the glass was a single piece and the dividers were simply struts fixed to the inside. The aluminium hard top was introduced in June 1956 and, according to Vanden Plas records, 1450 were made until June 1960. The second type of hard top was made by Universal Laminations in fibreglass and covered in black vinyl. It had a rather smaller rear window. It was introduced together with the 1600 model in May 1959; production figures are not known. Both types of hard top required special sliding sidescreens in aluminium frames.

The early aluminium hard top made by Vanden Plas. Note the brackets which attach it to the hood retaining plates on the rear tonneau panel. The hard top is here shown with the aluminium frame sliding sidescreens – the correct combination.

This is the later-style fibreglass hard top. Without the sidescreen in place, the position of the tonneau cover fasteners on the door top is also clearly seen: three fasteners along the shoulder of the door, and the fourth in the very front corner of the door, below the grab handle.

Windscreen washer kit Tudor manual, with plastic bottle in mounting bracket (usually painted blue) on bulkhead shelf, on early 1500 models in front of heater, more often on the opposite side to the master cylinder. Various types of control may be found, mounted on the facia. Two jets were found on the scuttle, of either the fixed or the adjustable type. Some changes were made to the windscreen washer, see list of changepoints. Available on all models.

Sliding sidescreens In aluminium frames. There were two types, intended for use with either the first or the second type hard top, but they could also be supplied on their own. See section on weather equipment. Available on all models.

Badge bar A chrome-plated tubular bar to be fitted with brackets behind the front bumper overriders. It was curved in plan view to follow the line of the bumper. Available on all models.

Cigar lighter Supplied by Casco Tex. See section on facia and instruments. Available on all models from 1958 onwards.

Ash tray Finished in black enamel with a chrome-plated lid, to be fitted on the propeller shaft tunnel in front of the armrest. Available on all models.

Internal sun visors One or two as required, available only on coupé models. The sun visor was changed from car/chassis 81532 (1600) or 2061 (Twin Cam).

Competition de-luxe seats Available on all models from September 1958 but most commonly found on Twin Cam and De Luxe models. Same seats found on roadster and coupé cars. Because the seat slides were further apart they required different floor boards from standard. See section on interior trim and seats.

Headlamp flasher switch Lucas 23A, with relay Lucas SB40-1. Available on all models from 1959 onwards, but mainly offered for North American (and German?) markets. See section on facia and instruments.

Anti-roll bar Available on 1500 models from car/chassis 66575 and all later pushrod-engined cars. Fitted as standard on Twin

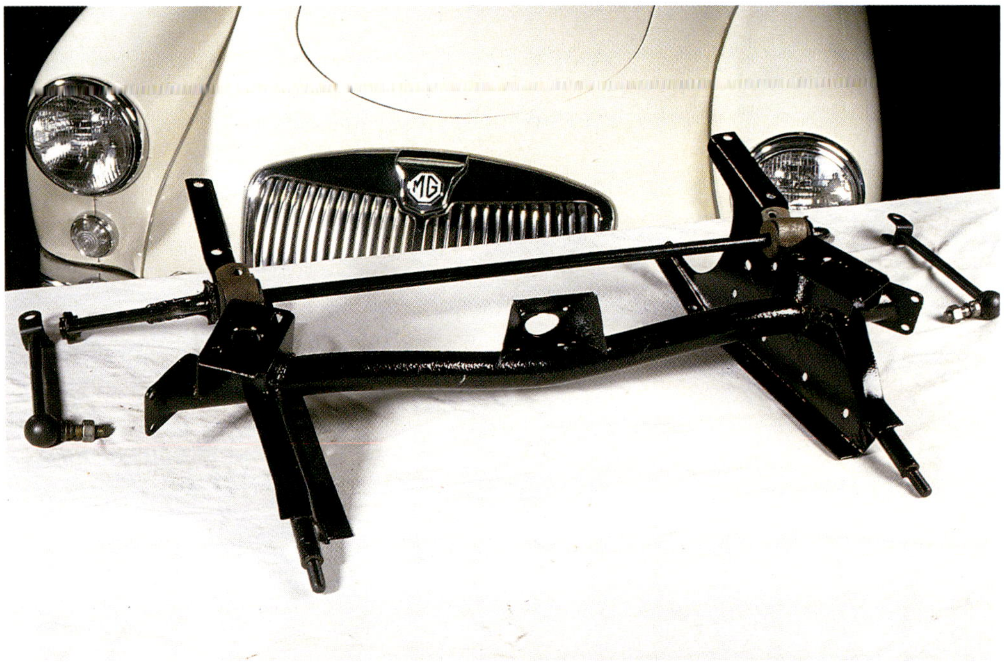

A chassis front extension complete with anti-roll bar and mountings.

The radiator muffettes offered by BMC for the MGA – the original type at the top and the modified type for the Mark II grille below.

Cam from car/chassis 2275, and on De Luxe models. Not to be fitted in conjunction with Andrex friction shock absorbers (cp. section on competition equipment). See section on front suspension.

Battery covers Supplied by Lucas. Introduced in April 1959 for all models.

Oil cooler Available on all models, and fitted as standard on 1600 Mark II export cars from car/chassis 102737. Sometimes listed as part of the competition equipment. The installation was different on the Twin Cam (where it was mounted further forward), and the connecting pipes were different on De Luxe models, but the same basic oil cooler was found on all cars from late 1958. (The type originally offered for the 1500 model was altogether different.)

Close-ratio gearbox Available on Twin Cam from April 1959 and also on pushrod-engined cars thereafter, but always most common on Twin Cam and De Luxe models. See section on gearbox. Gear cluster for conversion listed as competition equipment.

Light alloy wood rim steering wheel Although originally listed as a competition item, it was later also fitted to cars on the production line (especially Twin Cams). See steering section.

All-wheel Dunlop disc brakes in conjunction with centre-lock disc wheels and Road Speed tyres Standard on Twin Cam, optional on 1600 and 1600 Mark II models from car/chassis 91240 in April 1960 in conjunction with numerous other detail changes. Pushrod-engined cars with this option are known as the De Luxe models. Originally built to individual special orders only, but in the last few months of production larger batches were built for the USA. See production figure statistics.

Seat belts Never factory-fitted, but a dealer-installed accessory available on the 1600 Mark II, which incorporated seat belt mounting points. Earlier cars required mounting points to be added, and BMC made service kits available for this purpose. The seat belts were static three-point belts typically supplied under the BMC label. They were originally made by Britax (BMC part number AHH6122) but later by Kangol Magnet (BMC part number AHH7319). Britax seat belts were silver grey, and the Kangol belts were black.

Among other **dealer-installed accessories** were a Lucas long-range driving lamp, type SLR576, matching the fog lamp type SFT576, and various types of reversing lamp. There was a selection of seat covers, including mock-leopardskin designs and wool tartans. Made specially for the MGA was a radiator muffette, which was later reduced in size to suit the 1600 Mark II's modified grille. Two designs of alternative badge bars were available, fitting on to the radiator grille bars, but these were standard BMC items and not special to the MGA. Another standard BMC item was a supplementary tool kit, containing four double-ended open spanners, a pair of pliers, an adjustable spanner, a tubular box spanner and a tommy bar, and a Phillips screwdriver, supplied in a tool roll – useful on the later 1600 and 1600 Mark II models (see section on boot). Dealers could also supply an exhaust deflector with an MG badge, while the following items could be fitted by dealers as well as in the factory: luggage carrier, radiator blind, heater kit, high-note horn, fog lamp(s), windscreen washer and wing mirror(s).

RACING & COMPETITION EQUIPMENT

The items on this list were, in the main, never made generally available to the public and were not fitted on the production line, but were supplied on request to owners who wished to use their cars for competition

MBL 867, one of the 1955-56 works rally cars, shows extensive modifications compared to a standard car, including the fitting of a 20 gallon petrol tank with Le Mans type filler cap in the centre of the boot lid, 60 spoke wire wheels, bumpers omitted and different rear number plate mounting.

From the front, MBL 867 shows its Lucas Flamethrower spot lamp fitted in one half of the grille à la *1955 Le Mans cars. This hard top equipped car is fitted with aeroscreens because of its competition provenance: on the 1956 Mille Miglia it raced with aeroscreens only, but was driven to and from the event with the full windscreen in place as well.*

purposes. Equipment of this type could under certain circumstances be fitted to owners' cars in the competition department workshop at Abingdon.

Heavy-duty exhaust valves With Bright Ray hard faces. Available for 1500 and for 1600s to engine number 16GA/20846.

Larger inlet and exhaust valves Of the type found on the 1600 Mark II. Available for the 1600 only.

Stronger valve springs Available for all pushrod-engined cars, in several different combinations giving different lift pressures.

Larger carburettors 1¾in diameter, with special inlet manifold. Standard needle SY or KW, richer RF, weaker KW1; jet size .100in. Available for all pushrod-engined cars; 2in carburettors were available for the Twin Cam.

Flat-top pistons For a 9:1 compression ratio. These modified pistons were available for the 1500 model.

Raised-top pistons For a 10.1:1 compression ratio, with fully floating gudgeon pins and special connecting rods. Available for 1500.

Pistons For a compression ratio of 9.25:1, with fully floating gudgeon pins and special connecting rods. Available for 1600.

Thermostat by-pass blanking sleeve For use when thermostat not fitted. Available for all pushrod-engined cars.

Special polished cylinder head With matching manifolds, supplied by the Laystall Engineering Company Limited. Available for 1500.

Competition clutch assembly Type 8ARG (similar to the Twin Cam clutch). Available for all pushrod-engined cars.

Alternative rear axle ratios Of 3.909:1 (11/43), available for all models; 4.1:1 (10/41), available for 1500, 1600 and Twin Cam but standard on 1600 Mark II; 4.875:1 (8/39), available for Twin Cam; and 5.125:1 (8/41), available for Twin Cam. Suitable speedometers were available for all these ratios, except the Twin Cam low ratio of 5.125:1. The 4.555:1 ratio was a normal production option (cp. section on options and extras).

Dunlop 60-spoke wire wheels Size 4½ J×15, with either aluminium alloy or steel rims. Available for all pushrod-engined cars, except the De Luxe.

20 gallon petrol tank Available for 1500 and Twin Cam.

15 gallon petrol tank Available for all models.

17 gallon petrol tank Available for 1600 and 1600 Mark II (from August 1961?).

Quick release fuel filler cap Le Mans type, available for all models.

Bonnet leather strap and buckle Usually supplied in pairs, available for all models.

Andrex friction front shock absorbers Available for all models except 1600 Mark II, but not to be fitted in conjunction with the front anti-roll bar.

High-setting hydraulic valves For front and rear shock absorbers, available for Twin Cam.

Competition brake shoes With Ferodo VG95/1 linings, or linings alone. Available for 1500.

Ferodo DS3 brake pads Available for Twin Cam.

Alternative camshaft For improved mid-range performance, part number 1H603 or 48G184, with valve timing 5°/45°/40°/ 10°, valve lift .322in and tappet clearance .015in. Available for 1500 and 1600. This camshaft was normally fitted to Riley One-Point-Five, 4/68 or 4/72 models. To be fitted together with an appropriate distributor.

Wide overlap racing camshaft Part number AEH714, with valve timing 24°/ 64°/59°/29° and valve lift .250in. Available for 1600 Mark II from January 1962. Also at this time, the factory advised that it was possible to raise the compression ratio of the 1600 Mark II engine to 9.8:1 by machining .040in from the cylinder head face, but such high compression heads do not appear to have been supplied by the company.

Higher output fuel pump Specification (part number) AUA73 (as Twin Cam), later AUF303. Available for all pushrod-engined cars.

Some items started out as competition equipment, but later became available as normal production options:

Close-ratio gearbox Or conversion kit including first motion shaft, laygear, second speed mainshaft gear and third speed mainshaft gear, with new second speed baulk ring as required. Available for all models. See gearbox section.

Oil cooler Standard on later 1600 Mark II export models. Available for all models. See section on options and extras.

Light alloy wood rim steering wheel Available for all models. See steering section.

A number of items were quoted only in the very first 1955 sales brochure but were never listed again. These included sodium core exhaust valves with bronze guides; bronze valve guides for standard exhaust valves; an unspecified competition camshaft; an extra fuel pump; and a rear axle ratio of 3.7:1 (11/41, or more accurately 3.727:1).

Aeroscreens and a Lucas Flamethrower spot lamp installed in one half of the radiator grille were found on some of the works cars but were never quoted as part of the competition equipment.

SPECIAL TUNING

The MG company issued a tuning booklet (reference number AKD819) giving details of five possible tuning stages for the MGA 1500 and MGA 1600 models, but does not seem to have issued any similar information relative to the 1600 Mark II models. The following are abbreviated extracts from this booklet, but any owner with a particular interest in these matters should obtain the complete booklet, which is available in reprinted form.

Stage MGA.1 (1500 and 1600) Tuning by polishing the cylinder head and ports for an increase of some 3bhp. Carburettor needles CC fitted if required on 1500 models. Should give 75bhp on 1500 engines or 82bhp on 1600 engines at 5750rpm.

Stage MGA.2 (1500 and 1600) Tuning for improved mid-range acceleration, by fitting camshaft part number 1H603 (later 48G184) from the Riley One-Point-Five, with valve timing of 5°/45°/40°/10° and valve lift of .322in, together with an appropriate distributor (from MG Magnette ZB or Riley One-Point-Five). Tappet setting .015in, static ignition setting 4° BTDC. This would produce an increase of 2-3bhp in the lower rev range, with the possibility of slightly impaired performance over 5000rpm. Could be combined with stage MGA.1.

Stage MGA.2A (1500 and 1600) As stage MGA.2, with the additional fitting of 9.0:1 flat top pistons (1500) or 9.25:1 pistons with fully floating gudgeon pins and special connecting rods (1600). Static ignition set at 4°-2° BTDC (1500), or 3°-1° BTDC (1600).

Stage MGA.3 (1500 and 1600) As stage MGA.1 with additional fitting of the 9.0:1 pistons (1500) or 9.25:1 pistons (1600). Ignition setting 4° BTDC. Carburettor needles CC (1500). N.3 plugs recommended for hard driving. Should give 78-80bhp (1500) or 85-86bhp (1600) at 6000rpm.

Stage MGA3A (1600 only) As stages MGA.1 and MGA.3, with additional fitting of the 1¾in carburettors with KW needles and special inlet manifold. Standard air cleaners modified to suit. Should give 88bhp at 6000rpm.

Stage MGA.4 (1500 only) As stage MGA.1 with additional fitting of the raised top 10.1:1 pistons with fully floating gudgeon pins and special connecting rods. Ignition setting 2° BTDC. Carburettor needles CC. N.3 plugs recommended for hard driving. Use of 100 octane fuel mandatory. Should give 86bhp at 6000rpm.

Stage MGA.4A (1500 only) As stage MGA.4, with additional fitting of the 1¾in carburettors with KW needles and special inlet manifold. Standard air cleaners modified to suit.

Stage MGA.5 (1600 only) As stage MGA.3A, with in addition combustion chambers reshaped and up to .030in machined off the cylinder head face to maintain a 9.25:1 compression ratio. Larger inlet and exhaust valves (as 1600 Mark II) to be fitted if required. Carburettor needles XF.

Standard distributor. Ignition timing 8° BTDC. Fan removed. Using 100 octane fuel, should give approximately 94bhp. Recommended only for special competition purposes.

It was possible to do many other things to the MGA engine, one well-known modification being the HRG cross-flow cylinder head with the carburettors on the right-hand side. A Peco supercharger conversion kit was also available.

Identification, Dating & Production Figures

All pushrod-engined MGAs shared one series of car/chassis numbers, while the Twin Cam had its own unique series of numbers. What MG called the 'car number' is normally called the 'chassis number' (US terminology: serial number) and which is now becoming known as the VIN (Vehicle Identification Number). Strictly speaking, if an MGA number is quoted complete with prefix, it is a 'car number', if quoted without prefix it is a 'chassis number'.

On the maker's plate, which is attached to the horizontal shelf behind the engine (and which may face towards either side of the car), it is known as 'car number'. This plate also has a space for the engine number but this was only used on early 1500s; on all later models it simply says 'see engine'. The car number without prefix may also be stamped into the chassis frame (see chassis frame section for details) or, in some export markets, may have been stamped in other locations by the importers. The car number plate is basically the same type on almost all cars. The exceptions are 1600 Mark II cars sold in Germany from at least June 1961 (these had a special plate which also quoted the permitted weights), and cars assembled in Australia (these had a BMC Australia plate giving the car/chassis number without prefix but followed by the 'Australian assembly number').

The pushrod-engined cars had the following series of car/chassis numbers: **MGA 1500** 10101 to 68850; **MGA 1600 (Mark I)** 68851 to 100351; **MGA 1600 Mark II** 100352 to 109070. The **Twin Cam** had the series of numbers 501 to 2611. The MGA 1500 number series started at 10101 for no other or better reason than that the previous MG sports car, the TF, had finished at 10100. The Twin Cam series began at 501 in accordance with common 1950s Nuffield practice.

This car number plate from an early 1956 car – in fact the prototype coupé – shows how the engine number was stamped on the plate on early cars. This is the correct position of the washer bottle on early 1500 models. There can be no doubt that this plate is original!

On this original early car number plate, the engine number is also stamped, with the first type prefix of BP15GB.

The car number prefixes on the 1500 model followed the contemporary Nuffield system, first seen on the TF (and Magnette ZA) models. These prefixes were composed of five characters – three letters and two numbers. MGA 1500 prefixes may be decoded as follows:

First letter Always **H**, for MGA model
Second letter Body type, either **D** for open two-seater or **M** for coupé
Third letter Class of colour. The following letters may be found:

- **A** Black
- **C** Red (found only on early cars), Orient Red
- **D** Blue; on roadster found on early cars only, Glacier Blue. Later Dark Blue; on coupé, Mineral Blue
- **E** Green (found only on early cars), Tyrolite Green
- **K** Light Red (from 1956 onwards), Orient Red
- **L** Light Blue (on roadsters from 1956 onwards), Glacier Blue
- **R** White, Old English White
- **T** Light Green (from 1956 onwards), Tyrolite/Island/Ash Green
- **H** Primer or CKD finish

First number Class of specification. The following may be found:

- **1** RHD, home market
- **2** RHD, export
- **3** LHD, export
- **4** LHD, North American export
- **5** RHD, CKD export
- **6** LHD, CKD export

Second number Type of paint. The following may be found:

- **3** Cellulose (lacquer)
- **5** Primer or CKD finish

On the 1600 and 1600 Mark II, the new

A much more pristine plate but still original, from a left-hand drive 1600 Mark II De Luxe roadster. The plate is the same type as found on the earlier car but has no engine number stamped in.

Two different engine number plates, both reverse-stamped and both rivetted, but note the slightly different styles of notation.

BMC car number prefix system was introduced, and these much less informative prefixes may be decoded as follows:

First letter Make of car: **G** means MG
Second letter Size of engine: **H** is between 1400 and 1999cc
Third letter Type of body: **N** is open two-seater, **D** is coupé
Fourth letter (if found) Variation from standard: **L** is left-hand drive
First number (1600 Mark II only) Model: **2** means Mark II

The Twin Cam had its own system, which was to some extent based on the original Nuffield system but in somewhat abbreviated form:

First letter Always **Y**, for MGA Twin Cam model
Second letter Body type, **D** for open two-seater or **M** for coupé
First number Class of specification. The following may be found:

1 RHD, home market
2 RHD, export
3 LHD, export (including North American cars)
5 RHD, CKD export (reported on cars in South Africa which have prefixes of YDH5 or YMH5, which uniquely incorporated the letter H for CKD finish)

There were five different engine types used in MGA cars, with different prefixes. Each series of engine numbers started with 101 (following BMC practice). They were as follows:

MGA 1500, to car/chassis 61503 BP15GB or 15GB-U-H, numbers from 101 to 51767
MGA 1500, from car/chassis 61504 15GD-U-H, numbers from 101 to 7816
MGA 1600 16GA-U-H or 16GA-U, numbers from 101 to 31660
MGA 1600 Mark II 16GC-U-H or 16GC-U-L, numbers from 101 to 8851
MGA Twin Cam 16GB-U, numbers from 101 to (estimated) 2272

In all engine number prefixes, the letter U would be replaced by the letters Da if a close-ratio gearbox was fitted by the factory.

Two different series of body numbers may be found. The first was used for all 1500 models and early Twin Cams with the 1500 type body. The second was used for 1600,

1600 Mark II and later Twin Cams with the 1600 type body. Because body numbers were not recorded by the factory at the time of production, the information that is available has been accumulated by taking numbers from cars later on. The following details are based on the work of Bill Gallihugh, Registrar of NAMGAR, to whom I am grateful for permission to reproduce them (see also *Safety Fast*, June 1991).

The 1500 and early Twin Cam body number series ran from 20001 to approximately 79000. These numbers did not have any prefix. The 1600/Mark II/late Twin Cam body number series ran from 101 to approximately 40600. These numbers were prefixed with the letter B.

Body numbers on Twin Cam cars were allocated in batches of 1000 numbers, each out of the main series, as follows. Early Twin Cams with 1500 type body: 61000 to 61999; 68000 to 68999; 76000 to 76999. Late Twin Cams with 1600 type body: 1000 to 1999. Twin Cam roadsters and coupés are mixed in these batches.

Pushrod-engined coupés also had body numbers allocated in batches of 1000 numbers each out of the main series, as follows. The 1500 coupés: 32000 to 32999; 42000 to 42999; 45000 to 45999; 49000 to 49999; 54000 to 54999; 68000 to 68999 (shared with Twin Cam bodies); 73000 to 73999. The 1600 and 1600 Mark II coupés: 1000 to 1999 (shared with Twin Cam bodies); 8000 to 8999; 19000 to 19999; 37000 to 37999 (this batch was used for Mark II coupés but some numbers within this batch were allocated to roadsters). Late 1600 coupés with car/chassis numbers over 92000 also seem to share their body numbers with the roadster series.

Evidently, not all of the Twin Cam or coupé body numbers were allocated, or were used on bodies for pushrod roadsters, as the numbers of bodies exceed the numbers of these cars produced (see production figure tables). CKD cars assembled abroad may not always have been issued with body numbers.

To enable easy dating of any MGA car, the accompanying table lists the first car/chassis numbers by year, together with other significant numbers and production dates, for pushrod-engined cars and Twin Cams.

MGA production figures have in broad terms been well-known for many years. In fact, MG made quite a splash when they made the 100,000th MGA in 1962. It is possible to get an accurate fix on overall production by simply subtracting the first from the last car/chassis number. However, the production figures have been refined in recent years. Graham Robson and I jointly identified and counted the De Luxe models in the production records, and I subsequently began counting the coupés as well (for which MG had never compiled separate figures). Counting Twin Cam and 1600 Mark II coupés was easy, but the bulk of this work was eventually done by Jonathan Stein (of *Automobile Quarterly* and the American MGA coupé register) who together with his wife Beki, spent three days in my office counting the coupés in the records. Their findings were originally published in *Automobile Quarterly* (vol.29, no.1) and are reproduced here with Jonathan's permission.

The figures are split in the groups originally used by MG's production control department. While no export figures by country have yet been found (although they most certainly were compiled by Nuffield Exports Limited at the time), the bulk of production was exported to the USA, where the MGA was the second best-selling British car until then (it was beaten by the Metropolitan). It should not, however, be assumed that all North American export cars went to the USA: Canada took quite a few, some were delivered in the UK on a tax-free personal export basis, while others were shipped to West Germany for US servicemen.

CKD (Completely Knocked Down) cars with right-hand drive were destined for Australia, South Africa or Eire. CKD cars with left-hand drive were destined for the Netherlands or Mexico. There may have been other overseas assembly locations that have yet to be identified. Some cars may have been shipped in what should more properly be called 'SKD' (Semi-Knocked Down) condition, including possibly cars to Cuba, the Philippines, Egypt and Brazil. The CKD coupés were mostly for South Africa (RHD cars) or Mexico (LHD cars). The Twin Cam was exported in CKD form to South Africa (RHD, roadsters and coupés), Eire (RHD roadsters), the Netherlands and Mexico (LHD roadsters).

The most important overseas MGA assemblers were: Australia – Nuffield (Australia) Pty Ltd, Zetland, New South Wales; South Africa – British Car Distributors Ltd, Durban, Natal; Eire – Booth Poole and Co Ltd, Dublin; The Netherlands – J J Molenaar's Automobilbedrijf NV, Amersfoort; Mexico – Automoviles Ingleses SA, Mexico City.

DATING AN MGA

Date	Car/chassis number	Notes
Pushrod-engined cars		
May 1955	10101	First MGA 1500
January 1956	11145	
September 1956	20671	First MGA 1500 coupé
January 1957	24609	
January 1958	45411	
January 1959	61117	
January 1959	61504	Introduction of 15GD-type engine
May 1959	68851	First MGA 1600
January 1960	82921	
April 1960	91240	First MGA 1600 De Luxe model
January 1961	99946	
March 1961	100352	First MGA 1600 Mark II
January 1962	106026	
May 1962	109070	Last MGA
Twin Cams		
April 1958	501	First MGA Twin Cam
January 1959	1030	
January 1960	2560	
May 1960	2611	Last MGA Twin Cam

Please note that the numbers quoted as the first numbers in each calendar year can only be approximate; there may always be a few cars with lower numbers built later, or with higher numbers built earlier.

PRODUCTION FIGURES TABLE 1

1500 ROADSTER

	RHD Home	RHD Export	LHD Export	LHD North American Export	RHD CKD	LHD CKD	Total
1955	210	93	106	594	0	0	1003
1956	794	721	1150	10589	48	92	13394
1957	368	379	1019	13869	672	160	16467
1958	368	349	848	12462	509	275	14811
1959	119	68	314	6149	142	11	6803
Total	1859	1610	3437	43663	1371	538	52478

1500 COUPÉ

1956	5	2	3	6	0	0	16
1957	398	182	198	3326	0	0	4104
1958	323	131	83	773	1	0	1311
1959	102	28	48	663	0	0	841
Total	828	343	332	4768	1	0	6272

1600 ROADSTER (INCLUDING DE LUXE MODELS)

1959	520	137	543	11378	248	112	12938
1960	780	271	1330	12253	764	80	15478
1961	34	41	42	37	136	24	314
Total	1334	449	1915	23668	1148	216	28730

1600 COUPÉ (INCLUDING DE LUXE MODELS)

1959	401	35	59	711	12	0	1218
1960	400	66	96	826	52	12	1452
1961	37	14	24	14	0	12	101
Total	838	115	179	1551	64	24	2771

1600 MARK II ROADSTER (INCLUDING DE LUXE MODELS)

1961	317	120	764	3921	84	48	5254
1962	60	39	392	2365	88	0	2944
Total	377	159	1156	6286	172	48	8198

1600 MARK II COUPÉ (INCLUDING DE LUXE MODELS)

1961	168	21	67	156	4	0	416
1962	51	10	18	26	0	0	105
Total	219	31	85	182	4	0	521

TWIN CAM ROADSTER

1958	39	41	144	256	12	1	493
1959	162*	127	208	679	56	24	1256
1960	9	7	2	5	4	12	39
Total	210	175	354	940	72	37	1788

*including one car delivered in chassis form (car/chs. no. 1701)

TWIN CAM COUPÉ

	RHD Home	RHD Export	LHD Export	LHD North American Export	RHD CKD	LHD CKD	Total
1958	26	7	5	10	0	0	48
1959	115	15	24	85	24	0	263
1960	9	2	1	0	0	0	12
Total	150	24	30	95	24	0	323

1600 DE LUXE ROADSTER

1960	16	2	32	0	–	–	50
1961	3	0	14	3	–	–	20
Total	19	2	46	3	–	–	70

1600 DE LUXE COUPÉ

1960	2	2	1	0	–	–	5
1961	5	1	0	1	–	–	7
Total	7	3	1	1	–	–	12

1600 MARK II DE LUXE ROADSTER

1961	12	6	22	77	–	–	117
1962	3	2	3	165	–	–	173
Total	15	8	25	242	–	–	290

1600 MARK II DE LUXE COUPÉ

1961	5	4	3	1	–	–	13
1962	8	0	1	1	–	–	10
Total	13	4	4	2	–	–	23

Total number of all De Luxe models: 395 cars

PRODUCTION FIGURES TABLE 2

	1500	Twin Cam	1600	1600 Mk. II	Total by year
1955	1003				1003
1956	13410				13410
1957	20571				20571
1958	16122	541			16663
1959	7644	1519	14156		23319
1960		51	16930		16981
1961			415	5670	6085
1962				3049	3049
Total	58750	2111	31501	8719	101081

COLOUR SCHEMES

No individual MGA model was ever available in more than six exterior paint colours, or with more than four main trim colours. Nevertheless, there is a surprising amount of variation, as will be evident from the tables in this section. First of all, most paint colours were offered with a choice of trim colours. Secondly, the roadster and coupé models were not originally offered in quite the same colour range. Thirdly, a major change to the colour list occurred with the introduction of the 1600 model in 1959, and this also affected the Twin Cam model. The 1500 coupé and early Twin Cam coupé models are particularly confusing in that they sometimes had two-tone interior trim colour schemes.

Frankly, not all of the MGA colours were well chosen. The most surprising omission was a decent British Racing Green. Instead, no fewer than three different pastel green colours were found in the 1500 and early Twin Cam range, while on later Twin Cams and 1600 models green was not offered at all. The blue colours also tended towards the lighter end of the spectrum with the exception of the original coupé colour of Mineral Blue. In the 1600 range, Alamo Beige and Dove Grey were both odd choices for a sports car. For these reasons, very many MGAs have been repainted in non-original colours, with British Racing Green and various dark red colours being favourites. At the time of production, the most popular colours were red and white, and these colours still predominate among original and restored cars to-day.

The original paints were supplied by Glasso or ICI. Original paint finish was cellulose (lacquer), with the important exception that the 1600 colour Iris Blue was synthetic (enamel), and on all cars the splash

COLOUR SCHEMES
1500 ROADSTER, TWIN CAM ROADSTER TO 2192

Paint, body	Paint, facia (1500 only)	Seats, armrest, casings, trim rolls, door seals, Twin Cam facia	Piping for seats, armrest, trim rolls and facia	Hood and sidescreens	Tonneau cover
Black	Red[1]	Red	Red	Black or Ice Blue	Black
Black	Green[1]	Green	Green	Black or Ice Blue	Black
Orient Red	Orient Red	Red	Red	Black	Black
Orient Red	Orient Red	Black	Red	Black	Black
Tyrolite Green or Ash Green	Tyrolite Green or Ash Green	Grey	Grey	Ice Blue or Black	Ice Blue or Black
Tyrolite Green or Ash Green	Tyrolite Green or Ash Green	Black	Green	Ice Blue or Black	Ice Blue or Black
Glacier Blue	Glacier Blue	Grey	Grey	Ice Blue or Black	Ice Blue or Black
Glacier Blue	Glacier Blue	Black	Grey[2]	Ice Blue or Black	Ice Blue or Black
Old English White	Old English White	Red	Red	Black	Black
Old English White	Old English White	Black	White	Black	Black

[1] Paint shades for painted facia on black 1500 roadsters are not certain. The 'Red' has been described as 'Cherry Red', and the green matched the trim colour.
[2] If fitted with competition de-luxe seats, seat piping may have been dark blue.

Notes
Black hood and sidescreens were rare on cars in Tyrolite Green or Glacier Blue. Ash Green cars always had black hood and sidescreens. Tyrolite Green was found only on 1500 roadsters until car/chassis 48333. Ash Green was found on 1500 roadsters from car/chassis 48980 in February 1958, and on Twin Cam from the start of production.

plates inside the front wings were finished in synthetic paint which had greater resistance to being chipped. Some paint suppliers' reference numbers appear in a table in this section.

Body colour paint was found inside the boot and in the engine bay, with the exception that the vertical toeboard support panel behind the engine was black as it was in effect part of the chassis assembly, and the chassis members showing in the engine bay were black. The insides of the wings were painted body colour. The battery cover panel or access hatch which formed the floor of the hood stowage compartment in the tonneau was body colour. On 1500 and 1600 roadsters, the facia panel was painted body colour, except on cars finished in black where the facia was painted to match the interior trim colour. The scuttle top on roadsters was painted body colour, except on the 1600 Mark II roadster where it was covered in red or black Novon plastic.

Some trim parts were the same colour on all cars regardless of paint colour. Thus, the roadster models invariably had black carpets and the coupé models had light grey carpets. Some very early roadsters may have had carpets colour-keyed to the interior trim colour (red, green and grey apart from black) and some early coupés may have had black carpets – but they were the exceptions to the rule. On coupés, the map pocket linings, the headlining, door top frame surrounds and trim found on screen pillars and screen top rail were off-white, while on 1600 and Mark II coupés (apart from late Twin Cam coupés) the rear quarter cappings behind the doors were also off-white. The spare wheel cover bag inside the car matched the carpet colour, while the spare wheel cover in the boot was always grey.

On all 1500s, the original colour may be

COLOUR SCHEMES
1500 COUPÉ, TWIN CAM COUPÉ TO 2291

Paint	Seats, armrest, door casings, scuttle casings, map pockets, rear quarter casings	Piping for seats, armrest and door casings	Facia, facia piping, door cappings, rear quarter cappings and parcel shelf rail	Scuttle top and parcel shelf	Facia trim roll	Door seals, piping for hinge pillar
Black	Red	Red	Black	Red	Black	Black
Black	Green	Green	Black	Green	Black	Black
Orient Red	Red	Red	Red	Red	Red	Red
Orient Red	Black	Red	Red	Black	Black	Black
Island Green or Ash Green	Grey	Grey	Green	Green[1]	Green[1]	Green
Island Green or Ash Green	Black	Green	Green	Black	Black	Black
Mineral Blue	Grey	Grey	Grey	Blue[1]	Blue[1]	Grey
Mineral Blue	Black	Blue	Blue	Black	Black	Black
Old English White	Red	Red	White	Red[1]	Red[1]	Red
Old English White	Black	White	White	Black[1]	Black[1]	Black

[1] The parcel shelf and the facia trim roll are also quoted in Grey and White in the Service Parts Lists. The parcel shelf and facia trim roll may have been grey on cars in Mineral Blue and Island or Ash Green with grey trim, and may have been white on cars in Old English White.

Notes
Island Green was found only on 1500 coupés until car/chassis 48178. Ash Green was found on 1500 coupés from car/chassis 49000 in February 1958, and on the Twin Cam from the start of production. Some early 1500 coupés were finished in the roadster colours of Tyrolite Green and Glacier Blue, but presumably with trim colours as indicated above for Island/Ash Green and Mineral Blue.

COLOUR SCHEMES
1600 ROADSTER, TWIN CAM ROADSTER FROM 2193, 1600 MARK II ROADSTER

Paint, body	Paint, facia (1600 only)	Seats, armrest, casings, trim rolls, facia on Twin Cam and Mark II	Piping for seats, armrest, trim rolls and facia	Door seals	Scuttle top (1600 Mark II only)	Hood and sidescreens, tonneau cover
Black	Beige (Alamo?)	Beige	Beige	Black	Black	Grey
Black	Red (Chariot?)	Red	Red	Red	Black	Grey
Chariot Red	Chariot Red	Red	Red	Red	Red	Beige
Chariot Red	Chariot Red	Beige	Beige	Red	Red	Beige
Chariot Red	Chariot Red	Black	Red	Red	Black	Grey
Iris Blue	Iris Blue	Black	Light Blue	Black	Black	Blue
Alamo Beige	Alamo Beige	Red	Red	Red	Red	Beige
Dove Grey	Dove Grey	Red	Red	Red	Red	Grey
Old English White	Old English White	Red	Red	Red	Red	Grey
Old English White	Old English White	Black	White[1]	Black	Black	Grey

[1] On 1600 Mark II roadsters from car/chassis 101490 in Old English White with black trim, the colour of the piping behind the facia trim roll was changed from white to black.

COLOUR SCHEMES
1600 COUPÉ, TWIN CAM COUPÉ FROM 2292, 1600 MARK II COUPÉ

Paint	Seats, armrest, casings, facia and facia trim roll, parcel shelf and rail, door cappings, scuttle top (1600 and Twin Cam models)	Scuttle top (1600 Mark II only)	Piping for seats, armrest, door casings, rear quarter cappings, facia and facia trim roll	Door seals
Black	Beige	Black	Beige	Black
Black	Red	Black	Red	Red
Chariot Red	Red	Red	Red	Red
Chariot Red	Beige	Red	Beige	Red
Chariot Red	Black	Black	Red	Red
Iris Blue	Black	Black	Light Blue	Black
Alamo Beige	Red	Red	Red	Red
Dove Grey	Red	Red	Red	Red
Old English White	Red	Red	Red	Red
Old English White	Black	Black	White[1]	Black

[1] On 1600 Mark II coupés from car/chassis 100596 in Old English White with black trim, the colour of the piping behind the facia trim roll was changed from white to black.

easily determined by reference to the car/chassis number prefix, which contains a letter denoting the class of colour (black, white, etc). For decoding, please refer to the earlier section dealing with identification. On Twin Cam, 1600 and 1600 Mark II models, there is no such convenient solution. If the original colour cannot be established in any other way, reference will have to be made to the production records.

A few MGAs were supplied in primer (an allowance was made on the purchase price!) to enable owners to have the cars sprayed in special colours, and a few cars were supplied from the factory in special colour orders. Witness, for instance, the very last Twin Cam which was finished in the TD colour of Woodland Green for original owner Mike Ellman-Brown, or the 100,000th MGA finished in metallic gold.

Although no data is to hand at the time of writing, it is perfectly possible that some of the MGAs assembled overseas were finished in different paint colours from those used on UK-built cars. This might particularly have been the case in Australia and South Africa.

PAINT COLOUR CODE REFERENCE TABLE

Colour name	BMC code	Glasso	ICI	Gipgloss/ Ault & Wiborg/ Berger	Dockers/ Pinchin Johnson	Ditzler/ PPG	Rinshed-Mason	Dupont
Black	BK.1	-	122	-	-	9000	-	99
Alamo Beige	BG.9	-	3343	21519	CHS 60	21973	9014	-
Glacier Blue	BU.4	5143	2984	17983	CHB 103	14035	-	-
Mineral Blue	BU.9	5329	3130	18921	CHB 84	15406	6600	8182
Iris Blue	BU.12	-	3243	20306	CHB 143	12235	BM.054	8184
Ash Green	GN.2	-	3221	20784	CHG 134	43376	-	-
Island Green	GN.6	-	2734	18329	CHG 62	44569	6614	-
Tyrolite Green	GN.7	5142	2985	17982	-	45291	-	-
Dove Grey	GR.26	5700	3346	21520	CHN 174	32085	6572	-
Orient Red	RD.3	5294	2935	18458	CHR 57	71609	-	-
Chariot Red	RD.16	5758	3344	21521	CHR 104	71420	9015 R	-
Old English White	WT.3	5324	2379	18580	CHW 8	8177	6642	8207

Notes

This table lists the original BMC paint codes and major UK/US paint manufacturers' codes (where available) to assist restorers wishing to order paint (with thanks to Caroline Robinson and John Twist of University Motors Limited, Grand Rapids, MI, for information on US paint manufacturers' code numbers).

Connolly's reference codes for the correct leather colours are as follows: Beige, 3555; Black, 8500; Green, 3368; Grey, 3371; Red, 3365.

ICI reference codes for Vynide leathercloth colours are as follows: Beige, CR.49/1610; Blue, BL.349; Green, GN.202/798; Grey, GY.70/795; Red, RE.138; White, WH.2. Black is known simply by the grain reference 176/238S, which is common for all colours. Leathercloth quality is either TXL.1A (seats and sidescreen pocket) or TXL.1B (other interior trim).

Reference codes for the Crossley's Karvel carpet colours are as follows: Black, KV.3033; Grey, KV.3159.

Reference codes for the hood colours on 1600 and other later models with Everflex hood material are: Beige, BE.5; Blue, BL.48; Grey, GY.2. The colour reference codes for the earlier cars with Vynide hood material are not known.

BUYING GUIDE

This unique car is the early 1956 coupé prototype, which was converted from a roadster and features a rear window style similar to the original hard top design. Apart from that, this car shows how badly affected by corrosion an MGA can become.

Most prospective MGA buyers would probably be very happy with any of the pushrod-engined models. There is very little difference between these cars in terms of performance or economy, but the higher rear axle ratio is an advantage of the 1600 Mark II. This and the 1600 also have the benefit of front disc brakes, although the drum brakes of the 1500 function perfectly well and require slightly less in the way of pedal pressure. The best compromise may be the 1600 model, which has disc brakes but avoids the slightly less pleasing radiator grille and rear lamps of the Mark II. On the debit side, the 1600 has the 'odd' engine size of 1588cc, not shared with any other B-series engined car, so certain engine spares may be more difficult to find.

Genuine De Luxe models take some finding and certainly command higher prices, but their attractions in terms of rarity and one-upmanship are not really accompanied by any practical advantages. They share the fiddly handbrake pad carriers with the Twin Cam. A Twin Cam should not be sought out simply because it is a faster car, and should be treated with sympathy and respect. Properly restored and maintained, the Twin Cam is as practical as any MGA – it just makes a few more demands of its owner. In terms of value, Twin Cams attract a hefty premium over pushrod-engined cars – the law of supply and demand at work again. In terms of enjoyment and pleasure of ownership, most people would not find it worth paying the extra for a Twin Cam.

The coupé is rarer than the roadster but less sought-after, fetching lower prices in a market obsessed with open-air motoring. But this model should not be overlooked, and offers obvious advantages in terms of all-year motoring. It is an attractive car in its own right, but the enclosed cockpit does make it a noisier and hotter car to drive. Those body and trim parts which are unique to the coupé are inevitably scarcer than equivalent roadster parts.

WHAT TO LOOK FOR

The most important area to assess when looking at an MGA is the condition of the bodywork and the chassis – corrosion is the great enemy. While the aluminium skins of bonnet, doors and boot lid are a help, the rest of the car is far from immune. The worst problems tend to occur in the combined door pillars and body sills – the F-sections. There is often little left of the bottom of the rear door pillar and the rear end of the sill, and the front of the sill where it joins the

Front view of the same car. Most of the missing parts, such as the front bumper, can be replaced with reproduction parts – if not always of absolutely the right design.

With the door hinge pillar in this state and the sill missing altogether, it is likely that the door simply fell off! Even in this condition, an MGA can be saved, but such a project would not normally be viable. However, the uniqueness and historical importance of this particular car will make it all worthwhile.

front door pillar can be so weakened that the body literally breaks in half when it is removed from the chassis.

Water will have entered from above, through the joints between shrouds and wings, and from below where mud thrown up by the wheels becomes trapped between inner and outer wings or between sill and chassis. The front inner wings and the splash panels are usually affected. The front wings rust towards the bottom in the area behind the wheels, and also behind the headlamps. The front shroud corrodes either side of the radiator grille, and the rear shroud typically decays at the bottom below the boot lid. The boot floor usually rusts through. All four wings are bolted on and some cars may have acquired fibreglass replacement wings at some stage. On coupés, the area where the roof meets rear shroud and wings is also susceptible to rust.

Apart from corrosion, many cars have suffered some accident damage which can affect almost any panel. Typical examples are front and rear end shunts, causing damage to the front shroud, valance, grille and radiator duct panel, or at the rear to the rear shroud and valance. A more severe accident may have caused body or chassis distortion. The workshop manual contains a useful diagram

Owned by Ian Wallace, this derelict 1600 coupé, with outer wings removed, shows how minor accident damage at the nose (a common occurrence) is often inexpertly 'repaired' with copious quantities of filler.

From within the engine bay, daylight shows extensive and typical perforation on the inner front wing behind the wheels, caused by water penetrating the shroud/wing joint from above, and by mud thrown up from the wheels. The chassis appears to be sound in this front area, as is normally the case on an MGA.

giving chassis dimensions, including the permitted tolerance on diagonals. Sadly, serious distortion sometimes only shows up when, mysteriously, it turns out to be impossible to achieve good panel fit during restoration, for instance when doors cannot be adjusted to give even shutlines. Even without accident damage or distortion, it can be difficult to achieve the correct 1/8in gap around the doors if all-new F-sections and front wings have been fitted. These components are available, as are all other body panels, but most replacement wings are not quite to the original shape and may require some modification to fit. Some otherwise very nicely restored cars have been seen sporting different front wings, with headlamps and sidelamps at different heights!

The worst chassis corrosion tends to occur in the centre section of the car, where water is more likely to have come in from above, particularly on roadsters. Of course, the wooden floorboards and the carpets are both highly hygroscopic. First to go are the floorboard rails and the battery cradles, but the side members and the cross member behind the seats may also be affected. The front end of the chassis is usually less prone to corrosion, being well protected by oil leaked from the engine, but stress-induced cracks may occur in the goalpost assembly. New battery cradles and repair kits for the floorboard rails and for the centre section of the main chassis frame are all available. Completely new chassis are not available but new re-manufactured bodies are – at a price.

Many MGAs have returned to the UK, or gone into Europe, from the USA in the past few years. The completely rust-free California car is a dream of many but such paragons are in reality quite rare, and any car which has lived in the south-western deserts may have suffered some rough and ready shot-blasting instead! Cars from other areas of the USA are likely to have rusted quite as much as UK or European cars. Ex-US cars are possibly also more likely to have suffered accident damage or to have been treated carelessly. They may feature a variety of mismatched panels or have very many non-original parts – such as the Metropolitan engines mentioned earlier in this book. Paint colours will have faded if exposed to Californian sun and leather also suffers the effect of sunlight. Many 'restored' American cars still seem to be retrimmed in Naugahyde or similar man-made materials – tough but

The combination of aluminium construction and a film of engine oil ensures that an MGA's bonnet survives well. Despite the advanced decay of the rest of this car, its bonnet is almost perfect – and the thick horsehair pad near the nose is still in place.

Two shots showing the contrast in corrosion potential of the steel front shroud and aluminium bonnet. On this car, dented steel at the nose has been built up with filler (top), while a line of filler along the outboard edge of the shroud (above) shows where fibreglass wings – often used for cheap repairs in the past – were crudely joined on. A previous owner of this car chose to obliterate the holes where the '1600' badge should be mounted, but the original chromed air vent grille (of the early variety without reinforcement for the transverse bars) survives intact.

unoriginal and unattractive. Cars are now being rescued out of US scrapyards and arrive as incomplete wrecks. Remember, the MGA was a 'banger' in the USA for longer than it was in the UK or Europe.

Two other considerations affect UK buyers of ex-US cars. The first is whether to convert to right-hand drive, which is simple enough to do as all the relevant parts are available, from steering racks to reproduction facia panels. However, one hopes that all converted cars offered for sale are described as such, and not passed off as original RHD cars. Unless the car/chassis number plate has been faked, it should be immediately obvious whether the car was originally RHD or LHD (see section on identification). Many UK owners will prefer a RHD car and in Australia RHD is a legal requirement. But if the dollar rate swings the other way, there could be a boom trade in converting cars back to LHD again!

The other point to bear in mind for UK buyers is that difficulties can now arise, with the DVLA having tightened up its system, over registration of an imported car which does not have a US title document (registration document). This applies particularly in those cases where cars have been found in scrapyards and brought over for restoration. Difficulties are also likely to arise when the Vehicle Identification Number (VIN) on the title document does not match the number found on the car. For some reason, many US title documents have the engine number listed as the VIN.

In purely mechanical terms, there is rather less to worry about. The B-series engine may be a trifle agricultural, but it is extremely robust and straightforward enough to rebuild. It tends to leak oil, especially from the rear of the crankshaft, and this will increase with wear. Another sign of ageing is increased tappet noise, and eventually some loss of oil pressure – which should be 20psi at idling, 50-60psi at normal running speeds. Cylinder heads also may crack.

The Twin Cam engine is a different matter altogether, and if the history of previous engine work cannot be satisfactorily established, it is recommended to have it checked by an expert. Twin Cam engines

The worst of the rust on the inner rear wings has occurred in the area where the splash panels would have been mounted. These two views show the same area from the outside (right) and from within the boot (left), whose floor has survived quite well.

Any MGA coupé is susceptible to rust where the roof meets the rear shroud, although only an extreme example will suffer this kind of collapse.

The worst chassis corrosion tends to occur in the cabin section of the car. With the F-sections cut away, gaping holes can be seen in the chassis side members, caused by mud becoming lodged in the finger-width gap between the chassis and the inner sills of the body.

can be rebuilt but it will be much more expensive than for a pushrod engine. A peculiar problem faces the owner of a Twin Cam which has been fitted with a pushrod engine – surplus Twin Cam engines are about as common as hens' teeth and a bit more valuable than gold dust.

Gearboxes become noisier with age and wear. The first and reverse gear clusters, which are straight-cut and have no synchromesh, tend to lead hard lives and in many cases these and the lay gear clusters are badly damaged and need replacing. The layshaft needle roller bearings are also a weak point. The second/third gear synchromesh baulk ring wears out, causing wear to the dog teeth on the gears, and the synchronizer hubs wear out. Worn gearboxes may jump out of third on the overrun. Perhaps surprisingly, the stocks of new gearbox spares are not very good, and at the time of writing new standard gear sets are not available – although new close-ratio gear sets are.

Rear axles also become noisy but very rarely give trouble. The front suspension swivel pins wear badly if greasing has been neglected, and may have seized to the trunnions if a car has been left standing. The front shock absorbers will almost certainly need rebuilding.

Exterior body trim parts, such as bumpers, are available in reproduction form, although not quite to the same shape as the originals – as illustrated earlier in this book. Remanufactured interior trim parts are also available, including complete seats if required. Most present-day replacement carpet is of too good (!) a quality, and is typically edge-bound where the original carpet was not, or has rubber heel mats of incorrect pattern. Carpeting is also available for the battery

A coupé door provides another example of the differing resilience of steel and aluminium. Although the door appears quite sound from the outside (above), water collecting within the door has devastated the base of the steel inner structure (above right). As this car's F-sections were collapsing through severe rust, a previous owner fitted a stout domestic bolt to keep this passenger door shut…

access hatch – but this should not be carpeted on roadster models. Another area where present-day owners may be tempted to 'gild the lily' is in the matter of hub caps, by fitting incorrect MG medallions. And inevitably, some people will insist on having chrome-plated wire wheels! For sheer practicality, there is actually a lot to be said for disc wheels – unless you really enjoy cleaning wire wheel spokes.

Many MGA owners have successfully completed restoration jobs at home from the most unpromising wrecks, but in general terms it would make sense for most prospective purchasers to go for the best car that is available within one's budget. With classic car values haven taking a tumble in the depressed early 1990s – partly due to too many 'new' ex-US cars chasing a diminishing number of buyers – it is now less likely than ever that restoration costs can be recouped if the finished car has to be sold. Almost all cars now coming on the market will already have had some work done, perhaps as much as 20 years ago when originality was not as important as most enthusiasts feel it is to-day. While this book should help you to judge the originality of an individual MGA's specification, the actual standard of workmanship of a car for sale should be very carefully scrutinized.

WHERE TO SEARCH

MGAs occupy the typical middle ground in the classic car market, where cars are offered in equal numbers by private vendors and dealers, with a substantial number also appearing in auctions. There will be several MGAs for sale in almost every issue of any classic car magazine. The most sensible move for anyone looking to buy an MGA would be to join one of the large MG clubs, where cars are advertised in the club magazines, and where help and advice can often be obtained from fellow club members or club officials.

This shot, taken from beneath another MGA chassis after shot-blasting, shows how the rails which support the wooden floorboards become eaten by rust, particularly on roadsters.

Providing that some disinterested advice is available to the less experienced enthusiast, buying a car privately can be the simplest and cheapest way. On the other hand, buying from a reputable dealer can offer greater peace of mind. The auctions are where you feel the pulse of the market most intimately, and while a few years ago MGAs at auction tended to be the cream of the crop and correspondingly expensive, there have been some surprising bargains to be had at recent auctions. But in the volatile classic car market, this could easily have changed by the time you read this…

CLUBS AND REGISTERS

The following are the most important clubs and registers for MGA owners, in the UK as well as the USA:

The MG Car Club Kimber House, PO Box 251, Abingdon, Oxfordshire OX14 1FF (tel 0235 555552). President, John Thornley OBE; Chairman, Ron Gammons; Administrator, Lyn Jeffrey. The oldest-established MG club, founded in 1930, the MG Car Club incorporates separate registers for the MGA and for the MGA Twin Cam. The club publishes the monthly *Safety Fast!* magazine, and has numerous local centres and affiliated clubs in the UK and around the world. Readers outside the UK and the USA seeking details of local clubs not listed here are invited to contact the UK-based MG Car Club headquarters for information.

MG Owners Club Freepost, Swavesey, Cambridge CB4 1BR (tel 0954 31125). Secretary, Roche Bentley. With 50,000 members, this is one of the largest organisations of its kind in the world. It offers extensive services to members and a monthly magazine, *Enjoying MG*. Many local centres of the club operate throughout the UK. With new club headquarters opened in the autumn of 1992, the MG Owners Club is in an excellent position to improve further its services to the benefit of its members.

North American MGA Register (NAMGAR) Bill Gallihugh, 2114 Pinehurst Drive, Carmel, IN 46032, USA. With 1500-plus members, this is the largest US club devoted exclusively to all MGAs. NAMGAR publishes a bi-monthly magazine, *MGA!*, and has more than 30 local chapters spread across most of the USA and Canada.

Apart from NAMGAR and regional MG clubs, the following specialized registers also operate in the USA:

MGA Twin Cam Registry Lyle F. York, PO Box 1068, Anderson, IN 46011.

MGA Coupé Register Jonathan Stein, 7450 Valley View Lane, Reading, PA 19606.

MGA De Luxe Register Rick Green, 412 Whitree Lane, Chesterfield, MO 63017.

Owners of MGA De Luxe cars are also invited to register their cars with: Jeff Wicks, House 5 Bella Vista, Lot 232 DD229, Silverstrand, Clearwater Bay, New Territories, Hong Kong.

Apart from clubs, the following two specialized magazines will be of interest to MGA owners and enthusiasts: *MG Enthusiast Magazine* (Editor, Martyn Wise), PO Box 11, Dewsbury, West Yorkshire WF12 7UZ (tel 0924 499261). *MG Magazine* (Managing Editor, Ron Embling), PO Box 321, Otego, NY 13825, USA (run in conjunction with *MG Magazine* are the informal M.G. Motorists Group and the Brit Books classic car book service).

Please note that the information quoted above is believed to be correct as of October 1992, but neither the author nor the publishers will be held liable for any errors or omissions or the consequences arising thereof, nor is any recommendation implied by the mention of an organisation or business in this section.